They Don't Hear Her Cries

ALETHEA GIBBS

This book consists of real-life situations in hopes to better your life and prevent you from making certain mistakes. Some characters and scenarios are fictional. Although the author has made every effort to ensure the accuracy and completeness of information contained in this book, the author assumes no responsibility for coincidental events.

They Don't Hear Her Cries
First paperback edition: April 2015

Editing by Linda Wilson and Antrina Richardson
Cover design by Mehdi Sohrabi Artworks

Library of Congress Control Number (LCCN): 2018910943

ISBN-13: 978-1-7327898-07
ISBN-10: 1732789800

DEDICATIONS

My motivation, my loves, my nieces; Ty-Janae and Ja-Tya, this book is dedicated to you. I want you to know that Auntie NeNe loves you beyond anything I can ever describe. This book is not something I want you to follow as an example but learn from and use as inspiration to be women of integrity. One day when you're older, I want you to read this book and understand that you deserve a better life. I want you to know that some of the things the characters experienced are the very things that I'm protecting you from. I also want you to know that you can do anything you put your minds to. I promise the possibilities are endless. This book is also dedicated to every woman who had to endure life without the presence of their father. You are not alone and with hard work, dedication, and forgiveness; you too will be successful.

HER STORY

Have you ever felt like your life was a mistake, or wondered what life would be like in another family? These thoughts replayed in Zenobia's adult mind over and over. Her mother had gotten pregnant with her at the age of twelve. Unfortunately for Zenobia, Mary didn't believe in having an abortion because she knew getting pregnant was one of the consequences of having unprotected sex.

It also didn't help that Mary never had a relationship with Zenobia's father. As the old saying goes, "Mary was young, dumb, and full of cum." Anyway, Zenobia's parents had a 'sex-ship'—they basically had casual sex and that was it. Obviously, that's how Zenobia came along, but Mary having casual sex didn't stop there. As the next few years passed, Mary had three more children, and they all had different fathers. None of the men stuck around to raise any of them. Mary's four children never had a father figure in their household.

See, getting a man wasn't Mary's problem; the issue was keeping him. But Mary had other problems that made things difficult for her children, such as being consistently single and unemployed. Men never took her seriously because she dated with her body instead of her mind. Also, Mary didn't have any employment for a few years because she often arrived late to work. Her financial status turned the men off.

Zenobia, the eldest child, didn't know everything, but she

knew what her mother was doing wasn't working. In fact, Mary's unwise decisions placed her children in harsh environments, such as living on numbered blocks like 21st Street, which was full of drugs and prostitutes, from Springfield Avenue to Clinton Avenue. Zenobia had watched so many drug transactions that one day she decided to steal marijuana from the local dealer's stash in the backyard. She wanted to find out what being high felt like, so she thought about using a little. But the rest she would sell and make a lot of money. On her way to execute her plan, she witnessed a male neighbor having sex with a cat. It freaked her out, so she rushed back home. For a while she heard the cat meowing in her dreams.

Essex County was the hood where Mary's children grew up, and to say it was hard was an understatement. Welcome to their world that was full of sex, money, drugs, gangs, and prostitutes. If you didn't agree with the lifestyle, there was a high chance of getting beat up, robbed, or killed on your block.

Instead of Zenobia enjoying life as a child or learning how to become a young woman, her mother Mary only had one lesson to teach: survival. Zenobia guessed it was what she had to do her entire life, but why did she and her siblings have to suffer for Mary's bad choices?

Although Shante and Rose were the younger sisters, and Pudge was the only boy, if you ever came into the Jordan household, you only heard one name being called. "Zenobia … Zenobia!" Mary claimed she was preparing Zenobia to take care of the family in case something happened to her. Well, Zenobia thought her mother just enjoyed picking on her.

Now that you know the background, here's Zenobia's story.

CHAPTER ONE

Fatherless Child

Zenobia always thought she was worthy of so much more in life, and she never understood why her mother's sex partner disowned her. Was she not good enough? Was she not pretty? What did she do to deserve her father's back? It's not like she didn't know who he was. She was very aware that her dad had other children and spent time with them. What she couldn't understand was why she never received any of that time.

Growing up, Zenobia did negative stuff because she was crying out for attention. Her father was alive, free, doing well, and therefore had no valid reason to disown her. His invisibility often left her baffled. Other than holding the title of "Daddy," he meant absolutely nothing to her. She didn't even know the man. Nor did she care about him and her mother maintaining a connection. Together or not, he should have been there for Zenobia.

The first time Zenobia was introduced to her birth father she was five years old, so her memory of him was somewhat blurred. The second time she met him, she was ten. Although it was five years later, she recognized his face instantly. At first, she assumed he was an out-of-town friend of Mary's. The truth was, as she watched television in the living room, she heard a male voice say, "Mary, I just need to see if Zenobia looks anything like me because last time I saw her, I was drunk and don't remember much."

"You are full of it with your sorry behind. Zenobia, come here because you have company."

Zenobia stopped watching cartoons and walked to the door as Mary went to the kitchen to cook.

"Hey, Mr. Man, I remember you."

The man laughed as he went inside the house.

"I know you do. I'm your Daddy, and my name is James."

Zenobia followed him inside. She put her hand to her chin.

"James? Then why don't I know you, and why you don't live with me then?"

Zenobia sat down on the brown sofa, but James never took a seat. He stood up the whole ten minutes he was inside. He kept looking Zenobia over carefully to see if she had any of his features.

"You're too young to understand, so I'll explain it when you get older."

"All right tell me when I get older."

James glanced around the living room.

"Well, it's time for me to go home. My ride will be here in two minutes. Let me get a hug. I'll see you soon though. I love you. Bye-bye."

Zenobia hugged her father. She was excited about the thought of seeing him soon.

"Okay, bye."

Shockingly, soon never came.

"Zee."

"Yes?"

"Did you get his number?"

"No, but I'll get it next time."

"Okay, and make sure you stay in touch with him because he's your father."

"Mom, that's my plan."

"Good, lock the door and get ready to take a bath. Tell Shante she's after you and Rose after her. I'll bathe Pudge once y'all finish. The spaghetti is almost done."

A few years later, Zenobia was headed to Irvington Public Library when she suddenly got nervous and her heart started beating faster. She knew that male face anywhere. James was standing in front of Irvington High School. Part of her wanted to pretend as if she were blind. *Just ignore him. Keep walking.* She thought it was too late to want him to play daddy since she was now a teenager. Fifteen to be exact. The other side of her, however, was full of questions, so she approached him respectfully and waved her hand to get his attention.

"Hey! Hey you!"

James was waiting at the bus stop, checking the bus schedule on his phone. An unbelievable amount of mixed feelings made Zenobia's head spin. She finally crossed the street and stood beside him.

"Hi."

"Hi," James replied as he looked up at her, caught off guard. His dark brown eyes widened. He was dressed in jeans, a gray hoodie, and work boots.

"Um, do you know who I am?"

"Yes, my daughter Zenobia."

Tears started to flow. She couldn't look him in the eyes. She kept looking down Clinton Avenue to see if his bus was coming. Zenobia wiped her face.

"Why did you say bye-bye to me five years ago? Why weren't you in my life? Why did you say you'll see me soon? Why did you lie with a serious face?"

"Zenobia, I—" he said, before being interrupted.

Zenobia knew she needed to talk fast because she wanted her questions answered before the 94-bus arrived. She folded her arms.

"Thanks to you, I don't use the word *bye* in my vocabulary anymore. Every time I hear it, I think about when you left me and never came back. I'm old enough to understand the answers to my questions now, and I'm all ears."

James shook his head shamefully. He wasn't ready for all the questions he'd just been hit with. He took a matchbook out his pocket and wrote his number down on the front piece then ripped it off the matches. He handed it to Zenobia.

"Man, I'm sorry, Zenobia. I was so young and afraid. Hell, I was just a child myself."

"I agree, you are sorry."

James looked down the street in search of his bus.

"Here's my number. Call me so we can go out this weekend, I'll explain everything to you then. I'll make it all up to you. I do want to be in your life now. Can you forgive me?"

Zenobia stared at James' hand. A second later she looked up at him, then back down to his hand as she thought, *should I take it.* Finally, Zenobia took the number and placed it in her back pocket.

"Yes, I forgive you because I want to get to know you."

James smirked.

"I'll be waiting for your call."

No matter how bad Zenobia felt about the strange man who had given her life, her mother Mary always reminded her, "James is your father, you have to forgive him and don't give up on him because we were young when we had you. I was only twelve and he was just fifteen. I know he's older than me, but women mature faster than men."

Zenobia would usually sigh, "Okay, Mom," because she didn't want Mary mad at her and accuse her of being disrespectful and ungrateful for talking back with disagreement.

The next day Zenobia contemplated if she should call her father or wait until another day. She wasn't sure of his availability and she didn't want her phone call going to his voicemail because she hated leaving voice messages. Despite her apprehension, she decided to call James. Zenobia dialed his digits. She was on a mission to finally have her father in her life.

"Please answer," she said aloud. The phone rang three times. A recorded voice answered.

"The subscriber you have dialed is not in service. If you feel you have received this message in error, please hang up and try your call again later. Message NJ six-two-nine eight-five." *Maybe I didn't dial the right number. Let me try it again,* she thought. Zenobia dialed again and heard the same recorded voice. Talk about tears. Her eyes filled quickly, and the tears fell nonstop. That same night before she went to bed, she felt the strong urge to pray. She got down on her knees, placed her hands together, and closed her eyes as she spoke loudly.

God, I don't like bothering you, but I have a question specifically for you that just won't leave my brain. If you know that my daddy means me no good, then why did you let James look into my eyes and lie to me again? I mean, right to my face. I just don't understand. Don't you know everything?

After that night, Zenobia cried almost every evening that year. From that day on she didn't believe a word out of anyone's mouth. She was mad at the world.

I hate everybody! Everybody is a liar, she thought. *If I can't trust my own father, then 'F' the universe!*

Zenobia's last memory of James was back in 2010. One day she had gone to Kim's Laundromat on Springfield Avenue by the post office in Irvington to wash clothes. There James stood alone, selling dollar socks. Zenobia put her clothes in the washing machine. She spilled some of the detergent rushing to catch James before he disappeared. She headed toward her dad with closed fists and stood directly in front of him.

"Hello, please don't lie to me because I can't take another lie from you. Why do you pop up at my house or in the area every five years with fabrications?"

James looked surprised to see his daughter standing before

him. His nostrils flared, and he stuttered.

"I-I-I—I'm so sorry."

Zenobia noticed the laundry workers and customers watching her. She opened her fists then shook her hands to prevent herself from punching James in his face.

"Yes, you are a sorry man—I mean *boy*—because you have a lot of maturing to do. I'm tired of hearing excuses when it comes to taking care of your responsibilities! My mother raised me without help from you. How about you tell the truth and stay in my life for once, or matter of fact, stay out because I'm over your games."

Everyone stopped what they were doing and focused their attention on Zenobia and James' dispute. James attempted to get rid of the stares aimed at them.

"Socks one dollar. Socks one dollar."

A few people kept gawking, but most went back to tending to their laundry. Zenobia didn't care who was watching. She had words to get out that she had been holding in for such a long time.

"Believe it or not, I don't say sorry anymore because of you. Instead, I say 'I apologize' or 'my fault.' I graduated from high school—class of 2007. Too bad you weren't there to support me."

James tilted his head slightly and sighed so lightly it was barely noticeable.

"It wasn't easy without you and I hated men for a while. I was even jealous of kids who had their fathers in their life."

Zenobia glared at James with so much rage and hurt bubbling up inside her.

"I didn't attend college because I didn't want you to miss another graduation of mine."

James scratched his head as he gathered his thoughts.

"Listen, I'm so sorry, Zenobia … I just don't know what to say anymore. I'm really proud of you and I want you to go to college. I … I—"

Zenobia interrupted him.

"There you go spreading your nostrils and stuttering because you're about to say some dishonest stuff. I know exactly when you're lying."

"Daughter, I need you to forgive me one last time."

James quickly gathered his merchandise. Zenobia guessed he was running away from the truth by heading to his next location to get money. A customer walked over to Zenobia.

"Go ahead, baby, forgive your daddy."

She gently patted Zenobia on the shoulder.

"Oh, by the way, you look just like him."

Zenobia turned and smiled at the lady. Then she placed both hands on her hips as she directed her mind back to her father, who was still gathering up his socks.

"Okay, I forgive you."

James slowed down picking up his stuff. He stared at Zenobia briefly.

"You do?"

Zenobia raised both eyebrows.

"Yeah. I'm giving you one last chance, but I'm not getting my hopes up too high because I honestly don't trust you."

James nodded. Zenobia shared her plans with him.

"I'll enroll in college next year. I want to study Psychology and get an understanding of hereditary traits. I'm going to take sociology classes, too. Also, I want to enroll in some business classes. I picture myself being the boss of my own company."

"Psychology, huh? I'm not into psychology or sociology because I got a lot of my father's bad ways. I guess that's why I wasn't in your life, but the business classes sound good because it's nothing like being the boss."

"Can you promise you'll watch me get my diploma?"

He placed his hands in his hoodie pockets.

"Yes."

"I'm not going to pressure you about visits and calls either. I'm going to speed up the process, especially for you. Meanwhile, I'll sacrifice my summer and take extra courses. Please save this date though. I'm begging you, do not let me down because I'm counting on you. By December 2014, I'll be a college graduate."

James scratched his nose. He then hugged Zenobia with both arms.

"Thank you. I love you. Sorry for the damage I caused, and I pr-pr-pr-promise I'll be at your graduation. Bye, Zenobia."

Full of hurt and pain, Zenobia couldn't hug him back.

"As always, I forgive you, but I need one more thing from you before you go on with your day."

He released her from his embrace. They stared at each other.

"What's that?"

"Please be upfront and tell me why you weren't in my life. I'm grown now, twenty as a matter of fact, so no more dishonesty."

"Fine, I'll keep it real with you."

"Good, because you are the main reason why I have trust issues. Why did you disown me and say I wasn't yours?"

James shrugged.

"I was scared, I didn't know what to do with a baby and I wasn't ready to give up my childhood."

Zenobia's tears fell.

"You're selfish. You didn't give up having sex though and had another child with another woman less than one year after I was born."

Zenobia wiped her tears.

"Another question I need to know, why did you make us take a blood test, but you never took yours?"

James picked up both bags of socks.

"Let me talk to you outside because I'm sick of these people in my business."

"Hold on because my machines stopped, so let me put my wet clothes in the dryers."

"Okay, I'll be outside because I need to smoke a cigarette."

After Zenobia threw her clothes in the dryers, she jogged outside because she didn't want James to get impatient. He stood there taking a hard long pull off his cigarette.

Zenobia cut straight to the chase.

"Mommy said for a fact that you're my father. I've been confused all my life. Shouldn't you have been there with us each time to take the blood test? How did you get away with it?"

James took one last long drag from his cigarette then tossed it in the street.

"You're my daughter and you look just like me. You even got my big nose."

Zenobia grinned slightly and rubbed her nose for a few seconds.

"I noticed."

"Look, I know I'm your father. I just owe you too much child support. I'm never going to pay it at all either."

"Stop it, I don't care about child support."

James stared somewhere far off and released a deep breath.

"I'll die first."

Zenobia couldn't respond. His words stung so bad that she let the silence speak for her. James broke her train of thought.

"So … I have a friend who works at the court. That's how I got away with it. She'll do anything for me, even lie and make the paper say you're not mine. If I took the test it woulda said I'm your father."

Zenobia stared at the sky for a second.

"That's not fair."

"Zenobia, life isn't fair. Keep it a hunnit. I'll do anything if it means I won't ever have to pay child support. I refuse to get a regular job because I don't want the government taking my money. By the time them crackers take out taxes and child support it'll look like I worked for free and I can't have that."

Zenobia wiped the sweat from her eyebrows as her blood pressure rose.

"Are you serious? I don't need any money from you. I make my own *money*. Besides, I survived this long without yours. I'm planning on selling drugs any day now because I want to know what it's like to have my own apartment. Minimum wage not going to cut it."

James shook his head and scrunched up his face briefly.

"What! You don't have to do anything illegal to get your own apartment. Did Mary ever tell you that I went to jail for selling drugs?"

Zenobia rolled her eyes.

"I already know you served time in jail for hustling, but I'll make sure I don't get caught like you did."

"You think it's so easy. It's rough out here, girl. I should know. Going to jail is no joke and neither is paying child support."

Zenobia grunted out her frustration.

"I don't want you to pay child support. I'll just write a letter for you and sign it, too. Real talk, we can go to the judge together. If they ever give me child support money, I'll give it all back to you, okay? Or will you do another no-show like you did during the blood tests? For the record, I'll always take love over money."

James didn't respond to that. Instead he picked up his two bags of socks off the ground, squinted, and gave Zenobia some parting advice.

"I didn't think I would get caught either, but I got greedy chasing that paper. Girl, I'm telling you now, jail ain't where you want to be. I suggest you do like me and sell dollar socks or something. Just take the path train to 33rd Street and walk towards 27th Street to buy your items wholesale, then sell them out here for profit."

Zenobia shrugged. Sadness overwhelmed her. Zenobia held her head down as if she'd lost all hope.

"I'll think about it because people love dollar socks. Well, until next time, take care. I need to take my clothes out the dryers."

James nodded.

"Cool. I need another cigarette and I need to go sell some more socks."

James walked away. Zenobia went back inside the laundromat.

All eyes were on Zenobia as she took her clothes out the dryers and started folding them. She couldn't take the pressure for too long, so she started folding faster. When she finished, she put her laundry bags in her trunk, then sat in the passenger side and pulled the seat all the way back. She burst into loud sobbing and chest-heaving cries.

Zenobia had a problem with the child support system. She knew firsthand how most of the time the child ended up suffering because of the father's inability to pay. Some men paid child support. Unfortunately, they didn't spend any time with their child. She guessed in the father's eyes it was one or the other. Some men disowned their child and would do anything to get out of paying child support. The thought made her sad, sick … she shook her head pitifully.

So, let me see if I have this right, the reason I don't know my father is because he doesn't want to pay child support. Wow … I don't know anything else to say … Wow!

Truth be told, she didn't want any money or materialistic things. Zenobia only wanted James' unconditional love. That was affordable. Yet, he didn't seem to want to make the investment.

Dear Diary,

One day I wish James would finally understand how much I missed out on because of his absence from my life. I never participated in Daddy and Daughter Dance, or any father-daughter events. I'm living proof while parents think they're hurting each other by breaking up, the child suffers much more. I'm not saying parents should stay in unhappy relationship. However, their child shouldn't miss out on a parent because of the breakup. I need my best friend. I'm tired of thinking about her. I know Shay been gone for a few years, but it seems like it was just yesterday. My heart is broken from the unexpected loss of my only true friend. Shay was more like my sister and could relate to me so well because she was raised without her father, too. We both knew some people would never understand how it felt to grow up with only one parent. We didn't admit it to anyone else. Meanwhile, we know every child need both parents in their life as two heroes to look up to. If one parent isn't around, then the child should be able to run to the other. Sadly, the only other option for some children is the streets in most single-parent homes. I still can't believe Shay was murdered. I want to vent to her so bad.

CHAPTER TWO

Looking Back

Zenobia was happy at Rutgers University in Newark, New Jersey until her junior year, because that's when she attended her psychology class, which hit close to home. Taking that course was like pouring salt on her open wounds. The first time Zenobia vented in class about James, her professor made psychological excuses as to why James was an absent father. Zenobia was told it was because of what her father experienced and was taught as a child from his parents. She had learned that during the child development stage, children mimic what their parents say and do. That class drained her mentally. One day she was so hurt she went to her dorm room after psychology class and cried hysterically. That night, Zenobia went to sleep thinking about not only her father's absence, but also the grueling absence of her best friend.

Shay, I miss you so much. I remember the secrets we shared. I wish you were here to talk to me. I love you, Shay. Good night.

Zenobia was sniveling at the memories of her most trusted friend. Her roommate Sylvia heard the outburst. She muted the television and then rushed to Zenobia's side of the room.

"Are you okay, girl? Do you need some tissue?"

Zenobia sniffled.

"I'll be okay and no, I don't need any tissue."

"Are you sure? Do you want to talk?"

Zenobia pulled the sheet over her head and stated, "For the last time, I'll be okay, so go back on your side and finish watching TV. Good night."

"My night will only be a good one if you stop having those bad dreams, or whatever it is that you're crying about. I'm here if you need somebody to talk to."

"No thank you. I'm fine. Good night, Sylvia."

"All right. Now don't say I didn't try to help."

"I won't. Now good night!"

Zenobia tried to hold in her cries. Unfortunately, she couldn't contain them. Once she released every tear, she fell into a deep slumber, wondering if the horrific memories would ever end. Zenobia screamed as she tossed and turned.

"They shot Shay and she's dead!"

The alarm app buzzed loudly. Zenobia jolted straight up to the annoying sound. She had bugged eyes and her heart raced with fear. She was not sure what scared her more, her dream, or the loud noise from her cellular phone. For a few seconds she remained still until her heart rate returned to normal. Zenobia headed toward the bathroom at the same time as her roommate, who moved toward her with a curious yet shocked expression.

"Sylvia, what's wrong? Why do you always stare at me like that every morning when I wake up?"

Sylvia pointed to her chest.

"Zenobia, I should be asking you what's wrong. Who is Shay?"

"What? Where did that come from? Wait a minute, why are you in my personal business, Ms. Nosy?"

Silence took over the room. Sylvia was perplexed.

"You don't even know what you've been saying in your sleep, do you?"

Zenobia rushed to the bathroom and slammed the door. Meanwhile, Sylvia asked a question from outside the bathroom.

"Who is Shay?"

No answer from Zenobia.

After Sylvia heard the toilet flush, she asked again.

"Zenobia, who the heck is Shay?"

"Huh? Girl, I'm washing my hands. I can't hear you with the water running."

"Fine, keep me in suspense then. I don't care."

"Calm down … If you want to know about my dream, hold on. I have to brush my teeth and shower."

"Okay, don't forget. When you finish I'll be here waiting on you."

Fifteen minutes later, Sylvia stood at the bathroom door as soon as Zenobia made her exit.

"About time you're out of the bathroom."

Zenobia walked to her side of the dorm room.

"My fault, I had to clean every spot on my body. Did you see the sweat that was pouring down my face when I woke up?"

"Yeah, I did. That's why I want to know about Shay."

Sylvia followed Zenobia back into their small room furnished with two twin beds, two dressers, and two computer desks, which left them with limited space to walk around. She sat on her bed across from Zenobia's. Zenobia sat on her own bed to lotion her body, then she grabbed her clothes lying on her yellow pillow, which matched the comforter. She slid into her denim jeans and white T-shirt, ready to revisit the past.

"I don't talk about my bestie much because I miss her a lot."

"Ooooh! Shay was your best friend?"

"Yes, we met in the seventh grade. Shay and I became friends during the announcement of the father-daughter dance at school.

We were the only two students who were sad and didn't want to participate since we didn't have an active father in our life. We shared painful stories about how bad we wished our dads were around. Shay and I were closer than Mario and Luigi."

"Aww, that's cute, and sad at the same time. Tell me what went down with her."

Zenobia grabbed an apple from her computer desk and washed it off in the bathroom sink. She bit her apple as she sat at her computer desk.

"I heard you say they shot her. Can you tell me what happened—if it's not too much to ask?"

Zenobia kept looking at her apple, then at Sylvia, as if she wanted to throw it across the room at her. She took two more bites. The thought of Shay's death brought tears to her big brown eyes. Zenobia leaned forward as her dark brown dreadlocks fell to her shoulders. Her skeptical gaze met with Sylvia's anticipating stare.

"Are you writing a book about me? I'm asking because I don't like anyone questioning me and trying to get close to me. I don't need anyone using me for their school assignments either."

Zenobia put her socks on then pushed her feet into her white tennis shoes. She wiped away the two tears that fell. Sylvia stood up.

"Bitch, we're in this dorm room together. Matter of fact, if you ask me, we might as well get to know each other."

"Real talk make that your last time disrespecting me, or I'm going to show you a psycho bitch. Sit back down on your bed, too because I don't like the way you stood up."

Sylvia sat down.

"Look, I understand this is our first semester and we have to share this dorm room, but I don't want us coming back from summer break and still acting like complete strangers next semester."

Sylvia seemed cool and genuinely concerned, so Zenobia nodded in agreement and decided to share the cause of her nightmares.

"I hope after I pour my heart out to you, I'll get to sleep peacefully every night."

"Well, let it out. I'm ready to hear the details."

"That's what I'm trying to tell you if you stop rushing me. Now, Shay used to live in Irvington by the McDonald's on 18th Avenue with her mother, Ms. Rowland. She was the coolest person ever in high school. A mature, well-known young lady and her attitude was good, mixed with a little bad. Some of the girls were jealous of her because Shay was so beautiful. The envious females never had the guts to tell Shay how they felt, so most of them did petty things like flirt with her baby's father."

"Wait, so she was a teen mom?"

"Yeah. Shay had a baby at a young age, twelve to be exact. She was about to get kicked out of her mom's house for dating Anthony because he was five years older than her. Ms. Rowland had a change of heart though and she didn't want to disown her daughter. Her mother was hurt because she'd had Shay at twelve years old. I'm sure you know what I'm going to say next, she wanted Shay to be better than her."

Sylvia twirled her weave with her fingers as her eyes widened.

"Are you serious? Her mother had her that young?"

"My mother had me at the age of twelve, too. I guess that's another reason we related so well."

"Oh, damn! That's super-duper young."

"I admit, it is. So, Shay and I had a lot in common. Anyway, my bestie wanted a father figure so bad, that's how she fell in love with Anthony. She got pregnant her first-time having sex with him. I didn't like Anthony. He was no type of role model and he was always the cause of my best friend getting into fights and all types of drama."

"Uh-oh, did she really get shot? Um, is she dead?"

Zenobia put both hands on her face, stood up, then sat back down at her computer desk.

"Wow."

"What? Why are you looking at me like that?"

"Girl are you going to listen, or keep stopping me to ask questions?"

"My bad. Go ahead, Zenobia. I'm all ears."

"Good, because you better be lucky I'm being nice and sharing my personal business with you."

Zenobia's apple started turning brown. Meanwhile, she took one more bite then she tossed it in the garbage can next to the computer desk.

"Anyway, back in 2007, Shay and I used to take turns spending the night at each other's house. One day I spent the night at her house and when I woke up the next morning, I heard her mother, Ms. Rowland, yelling, 'Kee Kee, stop calling here playing on my phone. I told you Shay is sleep. I promise if you keep making threats, I'm going to have you arrested.'

"Ms. Rowland was frustrated and tossed her cordless phone on her red couch. I knew what was going on because Shay told me Anthony's ex-girlfriend had been playing on the house phone all week. I was about ready to take care of Kee Kee myself. I wanted to get permission from Ms. Rowland first that's why I asked, 'Should I call Shante and let her handle Kee Kee? This is getting out of hand now. Just a friendly reminder, this is considered stalking.'

"Of course, Ms. Rowland did not want to see my sister in jail. She stated, 'I'm shocked you're even entertaining this stuff. Since when you started tolerating Shante's thuggish lifestyle, Zenobia?'

"Ms. Rowland thought I was a responsible, positive high school student, so I just let her keep that image of me. I quickly explained, 'I don't condone anything she does. I'm just saying enough is enough though. Shante loves fighting. I've sat here quietly. Honest, I didn't get involved because the thug life isn't for me.'

'Well, act like it. Also, warn your sister about these streets because I don't want us having to prepare for her funeral.'

'But one day Kee Kee approached Shay because she told Anthony to stop talking to her. Your daughter beat her up when they had a fair fight. You can ask Shay when she gets up. Unfortunately, Kee Kee is planning to jump her. Now I think you should let Shante and a few others put hands on her before she gets to Shay first. I mean, two can play this game.'

"Ms. Rowland shook her head and confirmed, 'I'll ask Shay when she wakes up. God, I feel so bad for this generation. The government needs to bring prayer back in the school.'

'My generation can't handle losing, Ms. Rowland. If they don't win, they want to shoot because majority of them are punks. I love my best friend. I swear I never want anything bad to happen to her. I'll continue to pray though.'

"Ms. Rowland disagreed, 'No, someone has to change the cycle.'

"We went back and forth for about twenty minutes. I didn't want to disrespect Ms. Rowland, so I took a shower and got dressed because I had to go to my brother Pudge's ninth birthday party. It was at my uncle's house on Grove Street. I had an awesome time at the party. It got my mind off getting Kee Kee beat up. None of my family acted ghetto or argued at the party. Everyone had a blast. We hadn't had that much fun together since that party."

"Did Shay go with you?"

"No."

"Why not?"

"Shay didn't come because she was exhausted from Anthony's drama and she had to wait for her grandmother to drop her baby off. I kept calling to check up on her because I wanted to hear my best friend's voice since I had a weird feeling her boyfriend was going to cause her to go to jail or something. I sent her a text message, too in case she couldn't talk. After everyone sang happy birthday to Pudge, he opened all his presents, then I called Shay again because I was worried. I felt some type of way because she sounded frustrated, as if she was crying or just finished crying.

'Hey, Shay. What's up? You slept all morning.'

'Nothing ... Anthony keeps taking up for Kee Kee.'

'What!'

'Yeah. I been begging him to stop talking to her and to tell her to stop disrespecting the house. But he never did. Yet, he claims he's tired of arguing. Check this, he wants me to walk with him to get some Chinese food. Talking 'bout we can work this out.'

'Pudge's party is almost over. I'll come spend another night, so tell Anthony to order something over the phone and get it delivered instead.'

'I did tell him that, I even told him I don't feel like going outside because Kee Kee and her crew going to be out there starting trouble. I think Anthony likes to see me fight over him. He claims he miss me. That joker said he don't want to argue anymore either. Well, I'm over him because he doesn't protect me or provide for me like a man should. I'm too pretty to keep risking my life for him. Watch, I'm going to dump him once we get to the Chinese restaurant.'

'Okay. I'm begging you, Shay. Make sure you call me as soon as you get back in, to let me know you made it to the house safe.'

'Okay. I love you.'

"Shay hung up the phone then about two hours later, I took the 90-bus and transferred to the 1-bus at Grove Street and 18th Avenue back to Ms. Rowland's apartment. Once I pressed the button for my stop, I shook my head as I got closer to the bus stop. Too many police officers were posted right there. Instead of checking out the scene, I decided to mind my business once I got off the bus. It was normal to have a lot of cops on 18th Avenue all day and night, and especially by the Chinese spot and McDonald's. Once I arrived at Shay's house, I called the house phone since the doorbell was broken. As soon as Ms. Rowland opened the door, one of her neighbors came from behind and almost knocked me over. She was screaming and yelling so loud that we had no clue what the lady said the first time. Ms. Rowland wanted a better understanding, 'Baby, can you please calm down and repeat yourself?'

"The neighbor shouted."

'They shot Shay and she's dead! Oh my God! I'm so scared … I'm a key witness … I was right there. And her baby father, too, but he just stood there.'

"I have to let my back touch the wall for this. Oh my God! This getting crazy. Kee Kee and her crew were there, right?"

"Yes."

"Damn."

"Although we didn't want to believe the bad news, Ms. Rowland and I hauled butt to the crime scene. Police officers had the spot surrounded, so once we reached the location we ran under the yellow crime scene tape. When we made it to the restaurant door we were stopped immediately. The cops were on point about protecting the evidence from being tampered with. They made sure no civilians entered the restaurant. I was so angry. I witnessed my best friend laid out on the floor inside of the Chinese restaurant with her eyes opened. Shay was dead! Ms. Rowland shouted so loud and kept punching at the air. She almost hit every police officer in sight. I couldn't take another second of observing Shay's lifeless body, so I went into law enforcement mode. I added, 'Y'all see my best friend lying there dead! Why isn't she in a body bag?'

"A male cop responded, 'Ma'am, stand back.'

"I wasn't trying to hear that, so I started talking back, 'Get a sheet or something. What's wrong with y'all?'

"Then he raised his voice, 'Listen, ma'am, you must stand back.'

"I felt like a criminal justice major. Just know I had to spit facts because I wanted my pain felt, 'I bet if that was someone in blue, the cop would be covered—truth be told, the body would be gone by now for the autopsy.'

"Another cop intervened, 'Ma'am, please let us do our job.'

"Ms. Rowland did her best to be the bigger person, 'Baby, I need you to please listen to them.'

"Zenobia, I never heard anything like this."

"I had witnessed someone getting shot before, but sadly, my

best friend's death destroyed me mentally. My other half had been murdered. Her own baby's father set her up. Regretfully, I couldn't bring her back to life. The look on her face was like: 'please help me.' My heart dropped … I literally fainted. 'Til this day I wished Shay had gone to Pudge's party with me, or that I had gone back to her place earlier, then she would still be alive. Anthony always gave me a negative vibe. Real talk, I never had any respect for him. At times I fall asleep thinking about my bestie. Believe it or not, you're the first person who let me know that I talk in my sleep."

"That was sad as hell. It would be juicy drama if I was writing a book, but I'm not. That ain't me. I was just worried about your nightmares and crying spells at night."

"Thanks. My mouth getting dry, let me grab a bottle of water from my computer desk."

"How you drink hot water?"

"Stop, you almost made me choke. I enjoy it better this way without getting a brain freeze."

"You have a point because I hate getting a brain freeze, too. Well, it's crazy how far a girl will go for some dude who ain't even worth it. Did the neighbor say who murdered her?"

"Yes, she said Kee Kee."

"How much time Kee Kee serving?"

"Unfortunately, she didn't get a charge."

"Why not?"

"Because a few days later when we tried to find the neighbor to talk to the detective, she moved out of state. Also, the murder weapon was never found."

"Wow! That's not cool."

"Nope, not at all."

"I'm sorry to hear that, just understand that your best friend's death wasn't your fault. Maybe you'll be able to sleep better knowing that."

"You're making me cry. You're right though. He wasn't worth it. I hope I'll sleep better, but when my bestie was alive she helped me cope during my weak days of stressing over my absent father. I think about the efforts I made to try to have my daddy in my life. No matter how much I pretend I'm over trying and I'm healed—but deep down, I still want to build a relationship with him."

"I can only imagine. When was the last time you saw your pops?"

"Let me place my water on the computer desk before I spill it on the bed. Uh, 2010 was the last time."

"I hope you see him soon."

"Me too, thanks. Well, since we're on the subject I'll tell you another situation of betrayal that occurred during my sophomore year of high school at my god brother Raheem's barbershop."

"Okay, I'm still listening."

"Raheem was six years older than me and one of the big timers in the hood. He used to sell heroin, and instead of blowing his money on women and luxury cars, he decided to flip the drug money and use it for a good cause. Raheem opened two soul food restaurants, a barbershop, and three sneaker stores. He always gave back to the community. He gave all his childhood friends and family members jobs. His theory was: he had known those people for most of his life. He claimed they would always hold him down and have his back. Yet experts say it's the ones closest to you who will cross you first. Girl, if you don't close your mouth."

"My bad, I'm not used to hearing gossip like this."

"Anyway, on New Year's Eve 2004, all the workers were busy inside of the barbershop doing haircuts for the New Year's Eve party that everyone had been talking about for at least six months. Everyone had planned to be together to bring in 2005. That day was very busy. Everyone was at their stations except Faheem. Faheem is Raheem's twin brother. Nobody cared too much because he always started all the drama at the barbershop anyway. As the day winded down, Raheem let everyone go so they could get ready for the big event. Once he attempted to lock the front door, four men barged in with ski masks on their faces and handguns loaded."

"Why are you smiling?"

"Because you have both hands on your mouth like you're watching a scary movie or something."

"Okay, I'll try to keep my hands from my mouth. Don't tell me you got shot though. I'm happy you're still alive sharing your story with me."

"Just listen, I need to get this off my chest because stress kills."

"Okay, go ahead and continue."

"All right, the burglars demanded money. Raheem was the calm type who didn't like confrontation, so he gave them all the money he had on him. As soon as the guys were about to leave, another person entered the barbershop. He was extremely angry and yelled at the other four criminals."

"Damn it's …"

"Hold on, let me finish telling you."

"Okay, go ahead."

"That fifth man stated, 'Y'all 'posed to shoot him!'

"The four men said simultaneously, 'We got da money, so let's go.'

"Adamant about his words, the fifth man let off four rounds. All four bullets hit Raheem."

"Zenobia, I'm sorry to hear these sad stories about your past."

"It's okay, I need to let it out. One of the dudes accidentally snitched. 'Faheem, what da hell is wrong wit' you, man? 'Dat's yo' fuckin' twin!'

"Sylvia, what's the deep gasp for?"

"I'm shocked and can't believe this. Are you serious, how do you know the details?"

"Girl, if you don't let me get to the end."

"My bad, this junk is juicy."

"Anyway, when Faheem's name was revealed, everyone left the scene. Hold on, let me use the bathroom real quick."

"To answer your question, I was in the back the whole time waiting on Raheem to count the cash for closing. Normally it was Faheem's job, but since he didn't show up, Raheem had asked me to help count it for him instead. When Faheem and the other four scums ran out, I hurried and dialed 9-1-1. I did CPR to keep my god brother alive. However, his pulse was fading. I was beyond nervous. Once the ambulance arrived after what felt like forever, Raheem, surprisingly, was still holding on. Once he arrived at Beth Israel hospital in critical condition, I had to answer all the personal questions for him. I knew everything, but I pretended as if I didn't know exactly who robbed and shot Raheem because I wanted my own satisfaction. While I executed a plan for revenge, the peculiar thing was Faheem visited his brother every other day with his fake tears and phony plotting paybacks."

"Zenobia, this is deep."

"True, and it's about to get deeper because I knew Faheem was only there because he had to make sure Raheem didn't find out that his own brother shot him out of envy. I called him out on it, too because I felt some type of way about the situation, 'Fah, why do you come here every other day?'

'Zee, what do you mean? That's my fuckin' twin brother, that's why.'

'My fault, you're right dag … I wasn't thinking clear.'

'It's cool, I'm just waiting for bro to wake up and let me know who I gotta' kill.'

"Zenobia, this junk crazy. How could someone shoot their own twin?"

"Good question. The peculiar thing is, he thought I believed his fake tears and phony plotting paybacks. But back to the details … Raheem fought for his life for two months in the ICU, then he gave up and was pronounced dead two days later. Before we buried Raheem, I had an early morning meeting with Faheem at the hospital to prepare the funeral arrangements. While we were chopping it up about the home going, I made it clear he had to pay for everything, being that their parents died years ago."

"I see it was tough without either parent around."

"True, but I don't want to talk about their parents because they died of a drug overdose."

"Well, finish about what you told Faheem."

"I confronted him, 'Fah, I know how much Rah loved you. Yo, he used to tell me he did everything for your benefit. Of course, your greedy, ungrateful behind didn't see it like that though.'

"He was like, 'Yo, get outta' here wit' 'dat shit because I loved him more.'

"I said, 'Well, you're doing a bad job showing it because if you were at the shop that night, he'd still be alive. And um, you should step up to the plate and pay for his entire funeral service. You're the only one who knows where he stashed all his money. I had asked him during one of our heart to heart talks because I suggested he had to tell someone he trusted in case he needed bail money or something.'

"I feel like I'm watching a talk show or documentary. Damn, did you hurt his feelings?"

"I'm not sure and I don't care, but he didn't deny it and started twisting his beard. All he said was, 'Word, he trusted me more than I trust myself. Now we need to get out this hospital talking about that.'

"I remained at ease and agreed, 'I know so come on, let's get on the elevator.'

"He insisted, 'No, take the stairs and stop being lazy.'

"As we walked down the stairs I said, 'I'll ride to the funeral home with you and help you fill out all the paperwork, too. Matter of fact, we're going now. Afterward, we can go to a bar or lounge because I want to get in the house before dark. I'm not beat for the big crowds either, so I need my space. I don't even like people staring at me because in my head I think they're scheming on setting me up or something. Also, people take pictures and put it on social media without your permission, so I don't have time for that.'

"When we walked outside, I noticed he wasn't excited about the future since he added, 'You right about social media because modern technology about to control the world. This shit about to replace books. Folks not going to communicate much in person either. Hell, the robots going to take people jobs, too.'

"Once we approached his car I said, 'Come on, open the door so we can take care of the funeral arrangements then hang out at a bar or something.'

"Faheem followed my instructions. Once Fah started driving, I prepared him for the questions he'd have to answer, 'Listen, when we arrive, make sure you say bury and not cremate.'

"We didn't make it out the parking lot because he pulled over in another parking spot and slammed on brakes. Good thing I had my seatbelt on because I would have flown out the passenger front window."

"That's funny girl, thank God for seatbelts though."

"Exactly, because he was adamant, 'When I die, I'm getting cremated so ashes to ashes and dust to dust for my twin.'

"I questioned him to make sure, 'Are you serious? You don't want anyone to visit your grave?'

"He was certain and stated, 'No, don't even save my ashes. Throw them in Irvington and Newark park because I'm known in the hood.'

"Damn girl, he seems evil."

"More like guilty. Well, we debated about cremating or not then we agreed no ashes because Raheem was the hood celebrity and he deserved to have his people from all over going to the cemetery showing him love. Once we agreed with the burial, we headed to Perry Funeral Home. Next, it was time to get some alcohol in his system. I got back in the car with him because I didn't have my license yet. Before we pulled off, I let him know, 'Fah, now that we've handled that, let's go to Marlo's to clear our mind and relieve some stress.'

"Faheem agreed, 'Word, because I need mad drinks ASAP.'

"While we headed to the lounge, he got curious, 'Zee, who do you think had the balls to bust my little brother's ass like that?'

"Girl you going to make my eyes fall on the floor. I can't believe he asked you that!"

"You better stop opening your eyes that wide before they get stuck. I can't believe he asked me that either, so I pretended right along with him and played my role, 'Fah, I don't know, trust me, once I find out I'm going to aim right for the coward's head without asking any questions.'

'Nah, come get me and I'll body him.'

'No, I need to do it because I still can't believe this.'

'I can't believe it either.'

'Your brother kept saying 2005 was going to be the best year ever. I guess he's better in heaven so Happy New Year Raheem. Well, the streets talk, so the truth will come out soon.'

'You right about that.'

'I'm on a mission because I know how these thugs play. They'll show up to your brother's wake like they feel bad, yet, they want to see for a fact that their enemy is dead. I swear to God I want the person gone right now. Walahi, as you say, since you're Muslim now.'

"When we arrived, Faheem parked on Lyons Avenue. He turned the ignition off then pulled his beard. I know he thought about one or all of the four guys snitching on him when he agreed with me, 'Word, the streets talk. You don't have to say Walahi if you don't want since it's all the same to me, you say God and I say Allah.'

"Oh boy, it's annoying when people argue about religion."

"I agree Sylvia, that's why I had to put it to an end and let him know, 'We're not going to get deep with the religion talk because I don't agree with all of it, especially since it separates people. Sadly, most individuals believe their religion is better than the next. Religious folks always trying to convert someone to their beliefs.'

'You don't know … I stayed arguing with my twin because he's Christian. I promise he always thought he was better than me. I don't care if my little brother had all of the money, everyone know I had the honey dips.'

'I wish everyone recognize it's only one higher power with different names. That way everyone could get along. I know it'll never be a perfect world, so life goes on. Back to the subject, Fah.'

'Word, if you find out who bodied him, make sure you let me know.'

'Okay. Trust me I got you. Real talk, you'll be the only person I tell.'

'Cool, now let's go inside Marlo's so I can get my drink on.'

'Sure. Let me put my purse in your trunk first.'

"Let me grab a snicker bar from underneath my pillow. Zenobia, I'm curious, did you give him alcohol poisoning? What are you smiling about?"

"You are too much. Pay attention because I'm almost done. Once we entered the bar, Faheem immediately ordered a shot of Absolut Vodka. He was paranoid because he wasn't sure if the other four guys told he murdered his twin brother. His first shot teased him, so he purchased another shot. The second shot gave him a little buzz, then he ordered a shot of E&J VSOP."

"The bartender was a little concerned, 'Are you sure you want to mix light and dark?'

"Faheem was an alcoholic who didn't know his limit, but he told her, 'I'm a grown ass man. Yes, I'm sure.'

"The bartender didn't ask him another question and laughed out loud, 'Say no more, grown ass man, here you go.'

"She knew Faheem was bound to fall or throw up. Also, she kept making eye contact with me, then finally she offered me a drink., 'What can I get you to drink, darling? Wait, I need to see your ID first because you look really young.'

"I didn't want her to know I was underage, 'I don't drink alcohol, so I'll just have a bottle of water please.'

"Faheem stated, 'I'll take a double shot of that dark for the both of us.'

"Once the bartender placed Faheem's E&J in front of him, I put an ecstasy pill in his drink as she took an order from the next customer."

"Damn, I'm happy you didn't get caught. What's the wink for?"

"Me too. I winked because I'm happy I didn't get caught. That's why I rushed him to leave, 'Fah, hurry up and pay the lady and let's go. That's enough shots because I don't have my license or permit.'

'What? Why not?'

'I take my driver lessons this week. We need to make it to our next destination safely.'

'What? I thought this was the last spot because you wanted to go home before dark.'

'Oh boy just listen because it was a surprise. I didn't want to tell you earlier. Unfortunately, I don't think we'll make it to the other location now.'

"Let me finish this snicker because the chocolate melting. What surprise and what other spot? Yo, Zee, don't give me that blank stare. Honest, I want to know about the surprise and other spot, too."

"Stop being silly, girl, it was part of my set up to get him out the bar because he had too much liquor."

"I understand now. Stop laughing at me."

"Good, now let me hurry and get this over with."

"My fault, go ahead."

"So … I was like, 'Get your mind right because I don't know how to drive and you're under the influence, so you can't operate a vehicle.'

"He looked at me as if I spoke another language. I had to remind him I wasn't playing, 'Seriously Fah, we need to go, I'll be outside.'

'Say that then, just one more double shot of that dark for the road.'

'No, Fah.'

'Wait. Let me get a single shot, then we out.'

'Come on, because you're drunk and embarrassing.'

"The bartender looked at me because she wasn't going to serve him. I gave her a nod to let her know it was cool to give him the single shot."

"I need to eat another snicker. I'll need some popcorn soon. If you decide to write a book or make a movie about this, I'll gladly support you. All I want to know now is, did you let him drive? Why are you twisting you mouth to the side like that?"

"Because I can't believe you just asked that. Hell no, I didn't know how to drive until that day because I was forced to learn. Faheem couldn't walk a straight line, so I took his car keys out his pocket, then I helped him get to his car. I even closed the door for him, too. Afterward, I got my Coach handbag from his trunk. Before I started the ignition, fixed the mirrors, and put my seatbelt on, Faheem was sleep. I turned the heat on because I was cold from that late-night breeze. Then I drove to the park."

"You went to a park at night? I hope you didn't get raped."

"Yes, I drove to Irvington Park because it was down the street. No, I didn't get raped. I parked the car close by the pond. Next, I reached down into my pocketbook, grabbed my gloves and put them on. I went back into my purse for the .22 Raheem had given me about four months before he died. Finally, I was ready for war. I got out the car and moved a few feet away. I didn't want the blood to splash on me. From the driver's side, I shot four slugs into his left temple. I threw the burner in the water then I drove to Weequahic Park to dump his body because I didn't want it in the same spot as the gun."

"Oh no, let me throw these wrappers in the garbage. Did anyone call the cops?"

"Not sure, because I left his car there then hopped on the 37-bus and went right home. What's wrong? Sylvia? Sylvia, are you okay? Why you look scared?"

"Nothing, I'm just speechless."

"Cool, because that's basically the end and the next few days everyone was talking about Raheem's death and funeral. There wasn't much talk about Faheem, but a few folks figured he disappeared since he wasn't at the funeral and his brother can't defend him anymore. Truth be told, he had beef with a lot of people and plenty of them wanted him dead anyway, so he became irrelevant. You're still mute. I guess you ran out of questions because I feel like I'm talking to myself now. Why are you breathing hard?"

"I don't know."

"To cut a long story short, the cops didn't put too much effort into investigating Faheem's case because no one reported him missing and Raheem's was priority. The detectives knew if they ignored Raheem's case, then street justice would be served. I kept my mouth shut as I silently embraced my get-even award. No matter how much it haunted me and stayed on my conscience, I always told myself I'd take that secret to my grave before I turned myself in."

"What the hell, where my shoes at? My roommate a murder."

"Calm down. Where do you think you're going?"

"Out of here."

"Stay because it's too dark to go out by yourself."

"It's cool, I need some fresh air."

"Okay, don't ever say I'm a murdered again or I'll kill you because you're the only one I shared that with. I need to get a good night's sleep without thinking about any type of killings."

"Whatever, bye."

"Whatever then … I'm going to sleep, so don't wake me up when you get back."

CHAPTER THREE

Get Out

When Zenobia woke up, she noticed a letter from her college roommate.

Good morning, I couldn't sleep so I decided to go home early. You can keep everything I left. I'm transferring to another school next semester. I hope you slept well. Before I go, your secrets are safe with me.

Sylvia xoxo

Zenobia was missing her roommate so much that she was almost late to class. It was the last day of her third year of college.

"Enjoy your summer break and stay safe!"

Zenobia nodded.

"True, can't forget the stay safe part, Professor Teart."

The students laughed. Zenobia went to her dorm room to get some sleep. Once she woke up from her nap, she packed her belongings then went to her mother's house for summer break.

The moment Zenobia arrived home for summer break with a

large black suitcase at her side and a car filled with bags, boxes, and dorm room necessities, her mother Mary started lecturing her from the screen door.

"Hello, I almost didn't answer the door because I wasn't expecting any company."

Zenobia exhaled and tried her best to exude a smile.

"Hey, Mama, how are you?"

"Don't try to sweet talk me. This is it, Zenobia. Why didn't you stay at your school? Close your mouth and answer me."

Zenobia scratched her scalp and avoided her mother's eyes.

"I'm not taking any summer classes this year. I'll take extra courses next semester. Also, I miss my family. Honest, I didn't think it was a problem to come home."

"What are you jumping for?"

Zenobia shrugged.

"I thought you were coming out here to hit me."

Mary sighed deeply and placed her hand on her hip.

"No, I'm checking for mail. Anyway, why didn't you warn me that you were coming here? I use your room as storage now."

"Storage? I … Well, I didn't think about all that."

Mary turned away and checked the mailbox.

"Look, I'm unemployed, no more unemployment checks, and now I must apply for welfare until I get a new job. As you can see, I'm not going to be able to provide for you. You need to get a job or I'm going to ask you to move out of here. Either you start giving me some money for rent and food or get your own damn place."

"Well, can I come inside now?"

Mary held a couple of junk mail letters then let the mailbox door slam.

"Mama, can I come inside? I mean, I don't want to discuss this outside, but what happened to me living here for free if I'm still in school though? Some of your sister's children still live with them, and the sad part is they're way older than me."

"I bet that's been on your mind for a while, glad you found the courage to ask. Don't go there though, because I gave you that option back in 2007, during your senior year of high school, before Shay got murdered. Just keeping it real—I'm not my sisters, so don't compare me to them again."

Mary stared at Zenobia then she rolled her eyes.

"My concern is you. It's fucking 2013 now, so you're too damn grown to stay here for free. If you would have gone straight to college after high school, you would have graduated by now with a good career in your field, but you wanted to settle and work for minimum wage instead, then your boss fired you when you finally decided to go back to school and further your education."

"Mom, can I come in now?"

Mary held the door open for Zenobia then let it slam once she was barely inside.

"Get in here!"

Zenobia dragged the huge black suitcase across the shiny wood floor.

"Why didn't you encourage me to go straight to college?"

Mary bit down on her bottom lip.

"I dropped out of high school, so I was happy you at least graduated."

Mary eased closer to her daughter, staring into her eyes.

"Listen, you are not about to point fingers at me. I'm the mother and you are the child, in case you forgot. As a matter of fact, I don't have to explain this shit to you."

Sometimes Zenobia didn't understand where her mother's head was at when she spoke. Zenobia continued with her thoughts.

That's the problem, she never explains shit to me—she just does stuff that irritates me or hurts me.

Mary walked to the kitchen to get a glass of ice water then she went back to the living room and sat on the brown leather sofa next to Zenobia.

"What's wrong?"

"Nothing."

"I see something is wrong. Fix your face and tell me what's wrong."

Zenobia held her head down.

"I feel like you should be happy that I'm home since I wasn't here in quite a while. I haven't been here several months, but that's not the case. You're fussing today just like you usually do."

"The bottom line is, you can't live any fucking where for free! You must contribute to something around this damn house. You're just an educated fool."

Zenobia looked up at her mother then put her head back down. Those words hurt so badly, but Zenobia pretended they hadn't. She found a space on the cream-colored wall to glance at until Mary was done.

Mary took a few gulps of water and placed her glass back on the coaster. She looked Zenobia up and down and spoke in a calm voice.

"If you can't respect my rules, then get out."

This woman must hate me. "It's always something with you, Mama. I just got home and here you are talking about get out! I didn't even do anything to you or my siblings."

Zenobia closed her eyes and prayed hard.

Please let me find a decent job so I won't ever have to come back here. "I swear to God I can't wait to get some money, so I can move out!" Zenobia yelled as she opened her eyes.

"Good, me either. I advise you to stop swearing though."

"Mama, I have an idea. How about you get a job? Because whenever you're working, I can stay here for free if I'm in school, but when you're not working for whatever reason, you threaten me and say I need to get a job or get out."

Zenobia wondered, *is this Mama's way of getting money since she's out of work? Why does she feel like she gotta use me to bring in money?*

Those thoughts bought on other thoughts. Something was wrong with this picture.

"Wait a minute, I'm twenty-three and I'm still in school. You have a twenty-two-year-old daughter who doesn't work or attend school. So why didn't you tell Shante she better find a job or get out, huh?"

Zenobia kicked her suitcase. It rolled across the floor. She shot up from her seat and nearly jogged to catch it.

"I mean, why you always picking on me, Mama? Why are you so easy on Shante though?"

Mary pointed her finger in Zenobia's face just as she was sitting.

"When she turns twenty-three then you worry about it. Until then, I advise you to mind your fucking business and stay in a fucking child's place! Shante's been acting strange ever since those Bloods murdered her father, and I don't want to add extra stress on her. I pray none of you die in the streets like him. I need you to grow up and understand certain things. You're the oldest and your siblings are counting on you."

Mary pushed the side of Zenobia's head.

"Instead of questioning me, you need to go talk to your sister and cheer her up or something."

Zenobia frowned.

This some real bullshit. "I'm scared to ask another question because you might hit me again. I'm confused. Why is Shante mad, I mean she's never even met her dad."

"She thought he would visit one day, and now it's never going to happen, so have some sympathy."

Oh my God. This is straight up wack!

Mary kept going on and on about the same stuff. It sounded like blah, blah, blah to Zenobia. Either way, Zenobia needed a job, regardless if she stayed at home with Mary or if she got her own apartment. It's possible to live with someone for free, but how do you live by yourself for free? Someone needed to pay the bills, right? Deep down, Zenobia knew her mother was right about finding employment. Unfortunately, her pride had her feeling differently. Therefore, she refused to tell Mary the truth. She wasn't the type to save money, so she wasn't financially ready to move out into the real world—well, not out on her own yet. Instead of giving Mary the credit she deserved as a mother who was showing her tough love because the real world didn't care about anyone, Zenobia decided something had to change. Zenobia was hurt. She wished she could have spent a few nights over her father's house, or at least asked him for advice. Because she was mentally wounded, she felt like hurting Mary, too.

Tears slid down Zenobia's cheeks. She stood up and glared at Mary.

"I promise you I'm going to sell drugs 'cause I need to make some easy, fast money. I'll be able to get my own place then. I mean it, I'll never have to come back here another day in my life!"

Mary put her head down as she placed her hand on her forehead.

"Sit down!"

Mary lifted her head as Zenobia sat across from her on the other couch.

"You can do whatever the fuck you want, but trust me, you won't ever sell illegal shit in my house! Also, once your foolish ass goes to jail, you better not call me at all because I won't bail you out, visit, or write you. You just made my blood pressure go up. Where my pills at?"

Mary popped up from the sofa, glanced around the living room and found her purse on top of the television stand. She took her pressure pill with a long swallow of water. Finally, she finished the last sip and put the empty glass back on the end table.

"You know what? You cause me to curse a lot, but that's about to end. Damn, I can't believe you waited until now, at age twenty-three, to do childish teenager shit. I mean it. You better pray you don't die behind selling drugs."

"I'm not talking about selling crack, Mama. Weed is an herb. Big difference. It should be legal if you ask me. Mark my words, the government will make it legal in about five years."

Mary shook her head pitifully as she glanced at her daughter.

"I didn't ask you if weed should be legalized or not, but I'm telling you I better never catch it in here."

Zenobia laughed.

"Huh, you what? Listen, it's a known fact that the government would rather arrest people for selling it. I've never heard of anyone dying from weed. Better yet, I know plenty of people with illnesses who got cured thanks to the natural herb. Cannabis can treat cancer, post-traumatic stress disorder, you know PTSD, seizures, anxiety, glaucoma, and depression, which means no money for pharmaceutical companies."

Mary folded her arms.

"Don't play with me, child. I hope you know you'll need a gun dealing with that dangerous street life. Why do you want to be a thug all of a sudden? It's bad out there, Zenobia. Live by the gun, and you'll die by the gun. I'm telling you … I'm praying for you. I pray you get some sense in your head not now, but *right now*."

Zenobia rubbed her eye.

"But Ma, you're the one who wants me to move out of here so bad. So now I have to make a sacrifice to get out and do what I gotta do."

"Are you about to cry?"

Mary wiped away her daughter's tears.

"Fix your face. I don't want you to move out, Zenobia. The truth is, it's time though. I'm overprotective when it comes to my children, especially you, because you are my oldest. God forbid if something happens to me, I want you to be able to take care of Shante, Rose, and Pudge. I don't want you to make the same mistakes I made in life. Please trust me and understand I want the best for you. Unfortunately, I didn't have my parents to teach me. If someone had led me on the right path, I would have listened. I never told you this, but I witnessed my father kill my mother."

"Huh? I thought Grandma died of natural causes before I was

born, and that's why you were in foster care."

"I didn't know how to tell you the truth. Sadly, it was easier for me to make up a lie."

Zenobia inhaled and exhaled rapidly as she cried harder.

"I'm sorry, Zee. That's why I'm sharing the whole story with you now."

"Mom, this hurt—it reminds me of James lying to me all over again."

"Listen, from now on I'm going to be honest with you, even if it hurts, because we must have a better mother-daughter relationship. I need you to be a better person than I was. Some parents are jealous of their children, but I'm proud that you're in college and didn't have a baby yet."

Zenobia smiled, happy to hear something positive coming from her mother for a change. She wiped her face with the back of her hands.

"Okay, Mom, so what really happened with your parents?"

"Don't judge me, but I called the cops on your grandfather, and he is serving double life at Northern State Prison."

"I'm not judging you because I would have done the same thing."

"Good to know because one thing about me, I'm a fair person and I live by: right is right and wrong is wrong. I pressed charges on him, too because he threatened to murder me. I don't trust him around me, you, or your siblings. I refused to drop the charges because I didn't want any calls or letters from him either. I might as well share everything with you now before it's too late. I'm not sure what may happen to you because of your negative thoughts."

"What negative thoughts?"

"You've been thinking I pick on you and I guess talking about doing stuff I don't want you to do, like sell drugs, is your way of hurting me. That's your payback, right?"

"Oh, that's because I feel like you're too hard on me. God knows I do my best to make you happy. You're always reminding me about finishing school and not getting pregnant too early, like you."

"Look, Zee, tough love is all I know how to give you, because right now your vision is real blurry. Just the thought of you talkin' 'bout selling drugs … it still bothers me."

Zenobia laughed out loud.

"Ma, I'm not trying to hurt you. I'll try to communicate with you more versus getting defensive and thinking you're out to get me when you're actually helping me stay on the right path."

Mary released a sigh of relief and smiled. She glanced at Zenobia long and hard.

"All jokes aside, we need to communicate more, so let's try together … I have a lot to talk about."

"A lot like what?"

"I was going to abort you."

"I can't take anymore. I need to go write and clear my mind."

"Okay, go clear your mind."

"Thank you."

"We're going to talk about this later though."

"Okay, I just need a minute to myself."

Dear Diary,

I have seen a lot and I have been through a lot, but I never thought I would hear Mary threaten to kick me out.

Is this what life is about?

She could have said I'll be uncomfortable for a while on the couch.

I was almost homeless, no doubt.

I'm hurt, ouch.

CHAPTER FOUR

Survival

"Zee, your father wasn't ready for a child. Therefore, I didn't want to raise you by myself, so the easiest option was to abort you. Besides, it was challenging taking care of myself at twelve. I went from foster family to foster family and never had stability. Each foster parent felt bad for me then gave up on me because they were responsible for two children instead of one. I had a difficult life, and I don't want you, Shante, Rose, and Pudge to go through life like I did. I'm doing my best to prevent y'all from making the same mistakes as me. I gave up my childhood for you. For once in your life, I need you to open your eyes and ears."

Mary took Zenobia's chin and turned it in her direction.

"I need you to look at me and listen. You looked toward the window when you heard the word abort. I'm giving you the truth. This was my reality, my youth. On everything I love, it was hard and not a happy journey at all. You don't know what it's like being sent from place to place, never knowing if you're going to like your new family. I stayed worrying how somebody was going to treat me. That was a very stressful time in my life. I'm thankful that you'll never have to know what that's like. Don't get me wrong, I know you want James in your life, and I wish I could make it happen. Understand this, you must do what's best for you no matter who's in your life or not. Shante knows some bloods murdered her father. One day I need to tell Rose her father is in jail for child molestation, and a racist white cop who feared his own shadow murdered Pudge's daddy. I said that to say this, I'm happy all my children are alive and not behind bars. Everything else we'll get through it."

Zenobia had a weird feeling in her stomach.

"Me too."

"Anyway, it's time to learn discipline and be responsible for yourself, girl. I'm your mother, not your lover, so you can't spend the rest of your life here at home with me. You must get your own apartment ASAP. I don't want you getting too comfortable here."

Zenobia swallowed her spit.

"I understand. I finally get it."

"You sure? 'Cause I'm not convinced you do. Thank God I have a life insurance policy for your silly behind because I see you're going to have to learn the hard way."

"What you mean by that?"

"You already know. Zenobia, I know you like the back of my hand and child, you are one hardheaded daughter."

"Mom, I'm not always hardheaded."

"I'll tell you what—since you got laid off from work, what you need to do is apply for unemployment."

"It's not my fault that my old racist boss didn't think getting an education was important. He told me that if I quit school, he'd give me more hours and a dollar raise. I told him that quitting was not an option. Then he asked me to stay overtime and I refused, so he fired me."

"Well, you are unemployed and need money now."

Zenobia walked toward the front door.

"Okay, let me get this suitcase out your living room. Also, I need to get the rest of my bags, boxes, and dorm room stuff from the trunk and put it in Shante's room for now."

Zenobia went to her trunk to get her belongings. Afterward,

she placed her things in Shante's closet.

"Shante, what's going on?"

"Zee, I didn't know you were here! It's stressful without you because Mommy stay complaining about money."

"Whatever, you trying to make me think you miss me or something."

"I really do miss you."

"You miss me getting in trouble for you; now Mommy see it's been you leaving the lights and TV on at night and not me. Anyway, let me put this stuff in your closet."

"Go ahead."

"Thanks. Where Pudge at?"

"He's taking a nap."

"I'll watch a movie with him later then because he'll be up all night. Where Rose at?"

"I think she's next door at her friend's house. Zee, I want to watch a movie with you."

"No, I don't like watching movies with you because you talk too much."

"Do not."

"Girl bye, you talk during the whole movie."

"Whatever, I only ask questions if I'm not sure."

"I don't feel like watching a movie."

Shante threw her pink pillow off the bed.

"You never have time for me and it's starting to hurt my feelings."

Zenobia put her last item in the closet then walked to the bed and hugged Shante.

"We'll watch a movie when Pudge get up. Actually, we'll wait for Rose, too."

As stubborn as Zenobia was, she gave in and applied for unemployment. She did not want to continue to listen to Mary complain about money. Meanwhile, she realized she needed money to live. The process of applying for unemployment benefits was way too long. Zenobia wished it were a better system.

On Friday at 9:33 AM Zenobia went to the unemployment office. The line was outside of the building. *Ooh, hell no! I'm not standing in that line.* Zenobia didn't have enough patience to wait, so she went home and logged onto the website instead. She had to answer so many questions. Once the application was completed, she waited one month for the non-monetary telephone appointment. Zenobia thought the non-monetary interview was BS, a money-saving tactic by the state. The strategy worked because some people didn't save, so they could barely go a week without a paycheck, which forced them to get a new job or sell drugs versus waiting for unemployment. When the lady finally called her on Monday, they were on the phone for over an hour.

Zenobia was asked for certain dates that were listed on papers she received from her employer. The woman had the audacity to say, "Ms. Jordan, you are taking too long answering my questions."

Zenobia ignored her and continued looking for her termination papers.

"Ms. Jordan, you are using up someone else's time slot."

Zenobia was so upset she had to take a deep breath because she didn't want to get denied unemployment benefits.

"Ms. Jordan, other callers who are prepared are waiting to speak to me, so I can help them file for their benefits. You're prolonging this interview when you should have already had your paperwork in front of you."

She's pissing me off! Zenobia slapped her hand on her thigh.

"It's taking so long because you want specific dates, lady. Being that I don't know for sure, I'm really thinking about it and checking my paperwork versus telling you a lie."

"Thank you for your time, Zenobia Jordan. That's all the questions I have for you today. Wait five business days for a letter to come in the mail to see if you're approved or not."

Click!

Well, Tuesday, Wednesday, Thursday, and Friday came and left. Saturday and Sunday didn't count as a business day, so according to the countdown, Zenobia was expecting her big news the next day. On Monday, Zenobia sat on the porch and waited for the mail lady. Sadly, no envelope was addressed to her. *I guess that rep got mad at me about my response time to her questions. I was only trying to make sure the dates were correct.* That abrupt click that ended their previous phone call clued her in as well. Eighteen days later, the letter finally arrived. It read …

You are hereby notified that based upon the facts obtained and in accordance with the New Jersey unemployment compensation law, the deputy (named below) has determined that you are disqualified for benefits from Gateway Security.

Words can't explain how Zenobia felt when she read the bad news. She did not want to tell Mary about getting disqualified. *I can't believe they have the right to deny someone of their unemployment benefits that they worked years for. They wonder why some folks rob, steal, kill, and sell drugs.* Meanwhile, she followed the directions at the bottom of the page and wrote her appeal letter. She thought the system was unfair and was designed for black people to fail.

For a while, a source of income didn't exist. Zenobia had to think of a master plan since her bills were past due and the collection agencies called twenty-four seven. Red 1-800 and 1-866 numbers stayed in her missed call log because she stopped answering them. It was annoying repeating herself to bill collectors. They knew she had no money. Therefore, she couldn't afford to pay her debt. A few representatives asked her to borrow money from someone else. She was shocked and told them, "I don't know anyone who will loan me cash since I don't have a job to pay them back." They kept trying to pressure her to give them a payment she didn't have. It got so bad that they called Mary looking for her. It was one thing to have funds and not pay a bill, but then it's another to be broke and can't afford to pay a debt. Zenobia's phone was about to get disconnected. A part of her wanted to do something strange for some change. When she called T-Mobile, the automated machine said, "Right now you owe two hundred dollars and it's due June twenty-ninth. Of that amount, one hundred dollars has been past due for twenty-two days. Since your account is past due, in order to keep it active, we recommend you make a payment for the past due amount of one hundred dollars."

Zenobia felt so pitiful and worthless. As she thought of her cell phone bill and car insurance, she had almost forgotten about how much she loved to shop and look nice. One outfit usually costed her one hundred dollars. She was desperate for money.

Finally, she was approved for unemployment about four months later. Sadly, she had accumulated so many past due balances that her unemployment benefits weren't enough to cover her debts, so she needed a lot more money. Through it all, she still gave Mary sixty dollars every two weeks. Mary was so money hungry, and she complained too much. Of course, one hundred and twenty dollars every month still wasn't good enough for her.

Dear Diary,

This unemployment check is not cutting it. I need to hook up with a connect on my block to get my hustle on and sell some weed to make a quick come up. This is my neighborhood, so the drug dealers know me. I won't get in too deep. Besides, I'm a female; the cops won't catch on that quick. Once I make these ends meet, I'm done with it because I can't let Mommy find out.

POEM

Sacrifice

One job is not enough

A second job could be tough

Living check to check is a lot of stress

How do I get out of this mess

I don't really want to sell drugs

I just refuse to struggle

CHAPTER FIVE

The Hustle

Although Zenobia wasn't a gang member, financial stress caused her to think about hustling. She didn't like the idea of standing on the corner all day and all night. Meanwhile, she anticipated the lifestyle. For instance, the large amount of money she'll earn in a short amount of time. Yes, she understood it was against the law to sell marijuana, but her mind was focused on the consistent funds that would eliminate her financial problems since she knew many people who smoked. Therefore, Zenobia wasn't concerned about the consequences.

Always a hard worker, Zenobia had many jobs growing up: a cashier at Target, Walmart, Modell's, Old Navy, American Eagle, and H&M. Zenobia worked on campaign elections, too. She witnessed firsthand how politicians got paid to lie to voters and manipulated them by persuading the citizens to believe their agendas and take their word at face value. In addition to her political work, Zenobia was an order picker and packer for a plumbing warehouse. She cleaned airplanes for Prime Flight, she was also employed as a sorter at UPS. During her job as a security officer for Gateway Security, Zenobia made only eight dollars an hour, which was her last employer before she started selling marijuana. Zenobia used to envy the cool kids on the block because they had all the money, nice clothes, and sneakers. She decided: "Can't beat them, might as well join them." That's when she got bold and went outside to ask her neighbor questions about how he made his money.

"Danger."

"What's good wit' you?"

"I don't feel like yelling, come over here real quick."

A car was coming so Danger ran across the street.

"Yo, what up?"

"Where your parents work at?"

Danger pulled his fitted cap over his eyebrows.

"They don't work nowhere. My pops in jail for a body, and my momma on welfare. Why, why you bein' so nosy?"

Zenobia put her hands on her hips.

"Well, I see you always wearing fly clothes and shoes. Somebody buying it for you?

"No."

"Where you gettin' money from?"

"Yo, you askin' too many questions."

Zenobia took her hands off her hips.

"That's because I need money."

Danger shook his head.

"You not 'bout 'dat life."

Zenobia met his serious gaze with one of her own. Danger held the stare for a while.

"I'm tired of struggling though."

"A'ight bet. I'll hook you up wit' my boss, Shotgun."

Zenobia smiled.

"When?"

"Tomorrow cool wit' me."

"A'ight then, see you tomorrow!"

Zenobia jogged to the corner store then skipped home. She was so happy that she would be earning a better living. She couldn't wait until the following day and had trouble falling asleep that night. Her heart pounded. She couldn't keep still thinking that tomorrow offered her a better opportunity than any other job she ever had.

Zenobia arrived at Danger's house early the next morning. She banged on the door as if someone was chasing her. Danger peeked out the blinds. He opened the window to speak to Zenobia. He frowned as he wiped sleep out his eyes.

"What up?"

"What's taking your boy so long?"

Danger yawned.

"Relax, Zenobia. Chill! You twenty minutes early. Sit right there on that chair while I go get dressed. I'll be outside in a few."

Thirty minutes later, Danger went outside, looking fresh and clean. Zenobia gave Danger a once over and looked down at her watch.

"Well, he's late now. Are you sure he's still coming?"

Danger pointed at the approaching vehicle.

"Yo, calm down. He's right there."

Shotgun pulled up in a 2014 Mercedes-Benz CLS. Zenobia and Danger got inside the car and slammed the doors. Zenobia sat up front and Danger in the back.

Shotgun turned the music down.

"What up with y'all slamming my doors though?"

Danger leaned forward and patted Shotgun on his shoulder.

"What up? My bad my boy."

Shotgun shrugged his shoulders to get Danger's hand off his shoulder.

"Whatever young blood."

Zenobia looked the dark skin, bald headed muscular guy over as she admired his gold watch and diamond earring. She held out her hand for a shake as if she were at a job interview.

"Hello, I didn't realize my strength."

Shotgun glanced at her hand. Zenobia placed her hand down at her side because she felt embarrassed.

"My name is Shotgun 'cause dat's my favorite toy to play wit'. Welcome to training day. Here's a hunnit worth of bud and each bag is ten dollas'."

Shotgun passed her the bag. Zenobia took it and put it in her purse. He had her attention. All of it. Shotgun drove around the block.

"Once you sell your work, bring me sixty back and you keep da forty. Da faster you get rid of it, da faster you make extra money. Don't take any shorts. I don't care if anyone say it's only one dolla', tell 'em you need ten. Oh, most importantly, if you eva' bump into a clown name Trigger, don't do business wit' him 'cause he's my competition. You'll know who he is when you see him because he always wears a shirt or hat with his name on it. What's your name again?"

Zenobia zipped her handbag.

"Zenobia, well, call me Zee if you want."

Shotgun stopped at the STOP sign, glanced at Danger then focused his attention back to Zenobia as he pulled over and put the car in park.

"Zee, I'll neva' trust Trigger, ya heard?"

Zenobia nodded with excitement.

"Yes. Okay, I heard you."

Shotgun laughed as he put the car in drive and proceeded on the road back to Danger's house.

"Stop wit' all 'dat white people shit."

Zenobia looked around, wondering if someone hit Shotgun in his head.

"I never knew black people couldn't say yes. Anyway, when will I learn how to bag the marijuana myself?"

"Yo, where are you from talking white?"

"I'm from—"

Shotgun parked across the street from Danger's house and interrupted.

"Neva' mind, 'cause I don't really care anyway. Just take it easy, grasshopper."

Zenobia shrugged then opened the passenger door. A guy in a car headed down the street blew the horn. Zenobia slammed the door.

"Sorry for slamming your door. Why that clown driving that fast though?"

Shotgun got out the car for some fresh air.

"Just go. Get out my car, both of you."

Danger turned his body to look out the back window. Once the coast was clear he opened his door. Zenobia followed his lead and they went their separate ways.

"Well, I'll see you for more once I sell this."

"Zee, you better not slam my door again and if you ever get in my car, you better check to see if anyone coming down the street or you owe me sex."

Danger laughed.

"My boy, you wild for that."

Shotgun got back in the car and pulled off fast as he turned his music up to the max.

Zenobia was on a mission to make a lot of money because she wanted to fit in with the popular crowd and forget about the absence of her father. All her jobs put together didn't amount to the illegal money she made selling marijuana. That's why Zenobia didn't instantly think about calling it quits. Besides, she was never a quitter. Then again, she had to rethink that previous sentiment. She knew trouble would soon follow if she got too comfortable. Zenobia told herself that she just wanted to get in the game, then get out quickly. She wanted to pay off her outstanding credit card debt first. Then she'd graduate and pay off her college loans. Maybe then would be the perfect time to exit the game.

Oh, she'd forgotten another important thing. As soon as she saved the right amount of money, she'd move out of Mary's house and into her own place. That's when she would quit and put an end to living the risky fast life. Truth be told, it was easier said than done. Already she'd saved more than enough money and handled all her business. However, the hustle was addictive. It was something alluring about living the fast life and the money that came along with it. For some reason, Zenobia became accustomed to the lifestyle. She didn't like paying taxes, so what excited and pleased her most was the IRS not taking any of her money. Regrettably, no matter how bad Zenobia knew the hustle was, the benefits she reaped were so good to her during that period in her life.

Even though Mary told her that she couldn't sell drugs in her house, Zenobia still did. She figured that what Mary didn't know wouldn't hurt her. Besides, Mary knew best out of anyone how hardheaded her own flesh and blood daughter was. For some reason, Zenobia just didn't enjoy listening and was very rebellious. Mary, however, always proclaimed, "A hard head makes a soft ass." Indeed, she was correct because Zenobia had the softest behind ever. Oh well, if Mary ever found out, at least Zenobia had already warned her. It wasn't her fault if Mary didn't believe her earlier threat about selling marijuana.

Zenobia wished Mary wasn't so hard on her, especially about paying her rent. It bothered her a great deal because when she was working, she always helped Mary out with two hundred every month. When Zenobia only received two hundred every two weeks from unemployment, she didn't feel as though she should still have to give Mary anything.

Zenobia enjoyed getting her hair done by Danielle at Cut Creators. Danielle did her hair for fifty dollars every two weeks. Although she tried convincing Zenobia to get her hair re-twisted once a month, Zenobia's stubborn behind went twice a month anyway. Also, each month Zenobia had to pay seventy for her cell phone bill plus three hundred liability car insurance. Good thing she treated herself to a 1995 green Hyundai Accent when she graduated high school, which eliminated a car note. Zenobia was a high-risk driver with a lot of points on her license. Mary often stressed Zenobia out so bad that she got used to going for a ride. She listened to Tru Werdz blasting from the speakers. While doing so, Zenobia tended to speed, driving eighty in a forty-five mile per hour limit and one hundred on a sixty-five mile per hour highway. Many times, Zenobia got caught and received numerous speeding tickets and reckless driving misdemeanors from state troopers. She had so many points, the Department of Motor Vehicles sent her a letter stating that if she received one more moving violation, her driver's license would get suspended.

The first thing Zenobia did with the illegal money was purchase a black 2001 Acura CL Type S. Mary wasn't happy about Zenobia's vehicle.

"Zenobia, get up here now."

Zenobia walked slowly up the steps and peeked her head in Mary's bedroom.

"Yes."

Mary pointed to the window next to her bed.

"Get in here, who car is that in front of my house?"

Zenobia smiled.

"Oh, the shiny coupe is mine."

"Um, do you have a new job?"

Zenobia shrugged her shoulders.

"Mom, something like that."

Mary looked at the car from her window then back at Zenobia.

"What do you mean? Either you have a job, or you don't. I'm really trying to figure out how you purchased that car."

"Stop playing, it's only a 2001."

"No, you stop playing and tell me where you got the money

from."

"I work with Danger, so I get paid cash every day."

Mary stood up and raised her voice.

"What do you mean you work with him? Danger is not the type of person I want you hanging around. Besides, his name speaks for itself. Your street name better not be Hazard either."

Zenobia stormed to her room before Mary reached her.

"I'm tired of struggling. Unemployment is not cutting it at all."

"You better stay in your room, and stay away from Danger, too because he's full of trouble."

Dear Diary,

Why is my life so difficult? What can I do to get rid of the stress? I thought selling weed and making extra money would help my family financially. I never smoked before, but now I'm curious what it feels like being high because I need to calm my nerves. Dag, I don't even know how to roll a blunt. I was told, "Never get high off your own supply." I'll continue to listen to the advice. Also, I hate seeing people choking when they smoke, so I rather drink alcohol instead.

Dear Diary,

I'm back. I tried a big gulp of Olde English beer today, but it was disgusting. Also, I took a few sips of Mad Dog 20/20 and it tasted good, like juice. I ended up drinking half the bottle. The next day I added a shot of Grey Goose to my routine. Talk about a new enjoyment, I was so drunk it made me feel like all my problems were gone. The feeling was amazing. Instantly I became addicted. The only problem was that once I sobered up, I had to face reality. For some reason, I enjoy being inebriated.

POEM

Trying to get by

She worked hard to stay alive. She didn't have big muscles, but she was tired of the struggle which caused her to hustle

It was tough and rough, but she was ready to scuffle

She didn't want to do anything illegal

The government wasn't for us people

Unemployment was at an all-time high

Folks couldn't afford to stay fly

The system was designed for her to fail

They wanted her to stress and commit suicide then go to hell

If they didn't want her dead for sure they wanted her in jail

She knew one day it would storm with heavy rain

She had that fear in her veins

She wasn't about that negative lifestyle. She was just trying to get by

CHAPTER SIX

Escaping Reality

Zenobia hated being sober because the feeling of having no worries was priceless. Unfortunately, she had some scary moments where drinking and driving became terrifying. One day Zenobia was driving down Lyons Avenue when she heard a loud scream. *Oh no, I hope I didn't hit anyone*, she mumbled. She slammed on her brakes while her car skidded, and tires squealed. Once Zenobia came to a complete stop, she attempted to lean forward, forgetting she had her safety belt on. She removed her seat belt to cater to the person.

"I truly apologize. Are you okay?"

The individual was standing in front of Zenobia's car with each hand holding both eyes closed. Zenobia shut her car door then walked to the person.

"Hello, I didn't see you with all that black on. You screamed so loud I thought I hit you."

The pedestrian started crying.

"I wish you would have hit me instead of my dog, you alkie."

"Lady, I truly apologize. Listen, I'm not an alkie. I can't believe I hit your dog. What's your name?"

"My name is Keeshia. The hood knows I'm that Gemini who call it how I see it, alkie."

"Keeshia, I'm trying to be nice since I ran your dog over."

Keeshia stood on the hood of Zenobia's car.

"You trying to be nice? No, I'm trying to be nice by not calling Irvington on you. I smell the alcohol on your breath. Irvington would love to give you a DUI for drunk driving."

"Keeshia, you are right about my drunk driving. Please, do not call Irvington on me. I'll stop drinking tonight."

Zenobia didn't stop drinking that night. On another note, she gave up drinking two weeks later. In addition, the idea of a future failing liver and AA meetings worried her. Zenobia got help quickly and ended that unsafe alcoholic habit. During her meetings she learned that people are not addicted to alcohol and drugs; they're addicted to escaping reality. Their life appears great when they're drunk and high, so they rather not stay sober.

Severely disheartened with Mary's inconsiderate and ungrateful ways, Zenobia wanted to get away from her mother and into her own spot. She got tints on her car windows to have a little privacy during the marijuana transactions. She felt safer while sitting in her car versus standing outside. She couldn't keep too much weed in Mary's house without getting caught, so she kept most of the product in the trunk. Often Zenobia took chase with the cops, being that she had five percent tinted windows. Her tints were so dark they were illegal. It caused a lot of attention with the police. Zenobia used to get so many tickets for tinted windows that she didn't pull all the way over anymore. She just sped away from the officers every chance she got.

Zenobia had forgotten to pay her tickets, which caused her license to get suspended. Disobedient, she kept driving with the suspension anyway.

One day a cop car tried to pull her over on Avon Avenue and Chadwick Avenue. The squad car eased behind her as if he had been intentionally waiting for her.

"Dang! Where the heck this pig come from?"

Zenobia pulled over to the curb and let the police officer approach her vehicle. *I can't take a chance with this weed in my car.*

I'm not going to jail. As soon as he got to her driver door, she pulled off. He hadn't even asked for her license, insurance, and registration card. The officer raced back to his vehicle and gave chase.

I hate going to court, she thought as she pressed her foot down hard on the gas pedal. Zenobia believed that it was always such an inconvenience when it came to the system. She thought about how much money she would miss out on simply waiting one hour for the judge. She remembered waiting so long for the judge to get to her case because she pretended she didn't have any money for an attorney. Paying for a lawyer would have taken less time to handle the dilemma. Also, it took even longer if she had to wait until after lunch. The cop was still on her tail. At that point, Zenobia made her final decision. *I can't stop now. I'll have to go to court and deal with the delays and staring at the time all over again. I'm not doing it.* She drove forward, then made a left turn at the traffic light onto Bergen Street and increased her speed to 65 miles per hour. Once she reached Springfield Avenue, she made a hard-left turn toward Irvington, which put her on two wheels. She almost crashed. Her tires screeched like a stolen car being driven, and the smell of burnt rubber wafted up her nose. She looked ahead as the movie theater, store fronts, and apartment buildings flashed past her eyes. Once she got the car under control, she blasted Tru Werdz' song, "Open Your Eyes," then she pressed the accelerator, driving 80 miles per hour toward Grove Street. She didn't stop at any red lights. From her rearview, she noticed the cop had called for backup. Her heart pounded fiercely as if it would burst out of her chest if she didn't calm her breathing. The police sirens along with the red and blue lights in the rearview mirror increased her nerves. She pushed down on the gas pedal a little more until the speedometer read 100 miles per hour. She thought about parking the car at McDonald's on her left then making a run towards Ellis Avenue. Zenobia didn't want to drive to Irvington Center, so she slowed down once she passed Popeye's and the laundromat. She made a right turn on Grove Street. Once she reached the Berkley Terrace Apartments, she parked all the way in the back. She had gained a nice distance on the cops, so they didn't see where she had gone once she turned. Exiting the car, she walked to her uncle's house; he lived in the complex. The car chase both petrified and excited Zenobia, knowing she got away with speeding through Newark and Irvington. It was something about the adrenaline rush she got when she did something bad and knew better not to do it.

Zenobia rang the first-floor bell and knocked on the window. The front door was unlocked so she walked in the hall. She smelled the cigarette smoke coming from her uncle Joe's apartment. Zenobia heard Joe unlock both locks and she heard him remove the chain. Next, he opened the door and smiled at his niece.

"Hey child."

"Hi, Uncle Joe, I have to use the bathroom."

"Go ahead."

Zenobia walked inside and locked both doors behind her while the smell of cigarette smoke hit her nose as she went to the bathroom. After she flushed the toilet she washed her hands and splashed water on her face. She stared in the mirror and smiled. Finally, she turned the light off and made her way to the living room. She gave her uncle a kiss before she sat down.

"Uncle, I almost urinated on myself."

Simultaneously Zenobia's uncle inhaled the last of his cigarette smoke and coughed.

"Child, you better stop holding your urine."

"Okay I'll stop. Uncle, do you want me to go to the laundromat with you?"

"No, I went this morning. When I put my clothes in the dryer I walked to the liquor store for my scratch tickets."

Zenobia's brown eyes opened wide.

"Okay because I noticed your laundry cart by the closet. Did you win?"

Zenobia's uncle lit another cigarette.

"Yes, I won fifty dollars."

"I'm happy for you uncle."

He smiled.

"Thank you. I'll ask your mother to give me a ride to Supremo's tomorrow for some milk, eggs, butter, and water."

Zenobia rubbed her stomach.

"Speaking of food shopping, I need to go home and eat. I'll try to visit you soon. I love you, good night."

"Okay, I'm about to take a nap. I love you more, stay safe."

A week later, Zenobia received a letter in the mail affirming an arrest warrant because she failed to appear at court. Although she hated going to court, she knew she had to keep her freedom. While on her way to post bail, she decided to go to the tinted window spot first to remove the tints, just to be on the safe side. Zenobia didn't get to do either because a police officer turned on his lights, trying to pull her over. In her rearview, the wailing siren and flashing lights made her ease her foot off the accelerator. *Hell no! I'm not stopping! I am not going to jail. It's a pound of marijuana in the trunk.* Of course, she sped up and got away because she had mastered the art of driving, and she knew every turn in Irvington and Newark with her eyes closed. Part of her thought the car was bad luck because she received too many traffic violations, so she decided to purchase another car.

Zenobia's main goal was a new ride and a fresh start. She headed to the Kia dealership on Route 22, and after test driving a couple of cars, she went with the 2014 Kia Forte Koup. Having the most expensive car didn't concern her much. She told herself that once she signed the paperwork, she'd drive properly and wouldn't get pulled over again. She knew that driving was an absolute privilege, so she had to obey the laws. Besides, she didn't get along well with people and couldn't depend on public transportation. Now she was back in business and back on her grind.

CHAPTER SEVEN

Caught Up

Shotgun was mad Zenobia started slacking on the job. She came outside late and went home early, which messed business up because people took their money to a reliable person instead.

"Yo, get in da car."

Zenobia took a seat and kept one leg out the car.

"What's good?"

"Not you. Close my door, we need to talk."

Zenobia put her other leg in the car and slammed the door.

"What I tell you about slamming my fuckin' door? I noticed you been moving funny."

"What are you talking about?"

"For one, the streets always talking n' I started spying on you two weeks ago."

"Okay, I been out here less because I don't want to work for you the rest of my life."

Shotgun turned the ignition off.

"Yo, as long as I'm your connect you do as I say, so you better stop playin' wit' my money. I will kill you n' me right now 'cause I ain't got shit to live fo'. Fuck you n' da rest of da world! Get da hell outta my car n' don't slam my shit again."

When he said that, Zenobia knew he was crazy. She wanted to

get far away from him because Shotgun had some loose screws upstairs. She didn't want to be another statistic since she was told he had shot his own brother.

Punk, I do not want to work for you anymore, she thought when she left his car and closed the door. Deep down Zenobia knew his gun made him feel tough though. She always wanted to get someone to beat him up ever since he tried to pay her to have sex with him, but she doubted that Shotgun would use his fists, so it wouldn't be a fair fight. One thing she disliked is when people with money tried to buy and control her. She wasn't the type to give in that easily. Sad to say, but Zenobia was convinced the average person doesn't do anything from their heart. Nine times out of ten, it's always a hidden agenda behind someone's kindness. For example, the mother of an old friend of hers used to tell Zenobia everything she did for her daughter. The mother claimed her child didn't appreciate it. Zenobia listened and replied, "Okay, that's what parents are for. Congratulations, you did your job as her parent." Zenobia believed most folks did certain things for bragging rights. On that note, she did her best to keep her distance from those types of people. If it happened to be a family member, she wouldn't dare let them do anything for her because they would believe she owed them forever. That night she wrote a few lines of poetry before she went to bed.

Dear Diary,

POEM

Water gun

I wonder if Shotgun ever shot a real gun

He probably scared people with an airsoft gun

If he come between my money he'll get shot by a real gun

The sound of it going to cause him to urinate

Make him change his name to water gun

He'll know I do this for fun

CHAPTER EIGHT

In Too Deep

Zenobia went to the Wendy's off Chancellor Avenue by Valley Fair to get something to eat. She noticed Trigger standing in front of her.

"How are you, Trigger?"

Trigger didn't recognize the voice, so he turned around fast.

"Who are you?"

"I know of you from Shotgun."

Trigger squinted.

"Really?"

The cashier was ready to take Trigger's order.

"Welcome to Wendy's, how may I help you?"

Trigger turned back around, looked at the menu, and proceeded to place his order.

"Umm, let me get a crispy chicken sandwich, large fries, and large chocolate frosty. Oh, get her whatever she wants. You could eat with me, so we can talk business. Tell her what you about to get."

"Thank you. Hello, may I have a junior bacon cheeseburger, small order of fries, and medium vanilla frosty?"

"Does that complete your order?"

"Yes."

"Is this for here or to go?"

Trigger answered.

"We're eating here."

Trigger dug in his pocket for money, not waiting for the cashier to tell him the total.

"Here's twenty, keep the change."

The cashier smiled.

"Thank you so much. Here's your receipt and your order number is thirty-one."

Trigger waited for their food.

"Go grab us a seat and I'll be there."

"Okay."

Trigger watched to see which table Zenobia picked then he grabbed some napkins and condiments.

"Order number thirty-one."

The Wendy's employee repeated.

"Order number thirty-one."

Trigger looked at his receipt.

"That's me."

The employee handed him the food.

"Enjoy your meal, sir."

Trigger checked his bag to make sure everything was there.

"Thanks."

He joined Zenobia at the table.

"This yours."

Zenobia jumped. Trigger laughed until he sat down.

"My fault, I messed your daydream up."

Zenobia shook her head.

"It's okay, I have a lot on my mind."

Trigger took two big bites of his crispy chicken sandwich and drank some of his chocolate frosty.

"So, how do you know Shotgun?"

Zenobia took a bite of her junior bacon cheeseburger then ate a few French fries.

"I used to work for him."

She drank some of her vanilla frosty.

"When I first met him, he made it clear not to mess with you. His exact words were, 'If you eva' bump into a clown name Trigger, don't do business wit' him 'cause he's my competition.' For sure I see he was right about you wearing stuff with your name on it that's really how I knew it was you."

Trigger ate the last bit of his French fries and drank the last of his milk shake.

"Damn, that's crazy his lying ass still telling folks don't do business with me. I bet he told you he doesn't trust me. If anything, I don't trust him because I tried to make him my right hand and he stole from me."

Zenobia finished her food.

"Wow, he did say he'll never trust you, but he didn't tell me about the stealing part."

Trigger pressed the remote starter on his key chain.

"He'll never tell anyone the truth, but he can't hide it forever."

Zenobia looked outside.

"Wow, remote starters are cool!"

Trigger laughed and threw away their garbage.

"Umm, what are you waiting for? Let's go for a ride."

Zenobia's bright eyes widened.

"Okay."

Trigger held the door for Zenobia as they exited Wendy's. He got in his car and put his seatbelt on.

"Put your seatbelt on and let me know what's your next move with Shotgun."

Zenobia followed Trigger's command.

"I'm done with that loser and I want to get my hustle on with you because he's trying to mix business with pleasure."

Trigger made a right turn when he exited Wendy's parking lot. At the corner of Chancellor Avenue and Fabyan Place, he was stopped at the red light. That's when he banged both hands on the staring wheel.

"Damn, he always trying to fuck his females instead of getting money with them. Real talk, cats like him mess it up for good guys like me."

Once the traffic light changed to green, Trigger parked in front of the liquor store on the corner of Leslie Street.

"From this moment forward, I'm putting you under my wings."

Trigger pointed in the rearview mirror.

"You see them two dudes across the street coming out that store? They're my right and left hand, so if Shotgun disrespects you again, let me know and they'll handle it from there. Okay?"

Zenobia looked out the back window to get a better look at both guys.

"Yes."

Zenobia turned back around to Trigger.

"Thank you."

The two guys crossed the street and shook Trigger's hand.

"What's goodie dude?"

"Same shit just different tissue."

Both guys laughed.

"You stay with jokes."

The guys noticed someone in the passenger side, so they leaned over to get a better look inside from the driver side.

"You got a new hottie?"

Trigger opened his sunroof.

"Nah, she's our first lady, so make sure she's protected in our streets."

"Say no more, Boss."

Trigger closed the sunroof.

"I'm out. Get back to business and get out the street before someone hit y'all funny looking ass."

Both guys walked away laughing.

"I swear you stay clownin'. We 'bout to get some Wendy's then back to the money."

Trigger pulled off and took Zenobia to one more spot before he let her out his car.

"This my crib. Meet me here in the morning and we'll start working together."

Zenobia checked her surroundings.

"I know someone who used to live on this block. This Wainwright Street, right?

"Yeah."

"Cool, what time should I arrive?"

Trigger took a moment to decide.

"Uhhh, eleven is cool."

"Okay, I'll meet you here."

The next day Zenobia rang the doorbell with a big smile.

"Good morning, I'm ready Boss Man."

Trigger shielded his eyes from the light.

"Good morning, get in here and stop calling me that because I'm about to teach you how to be the boss."

Trigger closed the door after Zenobia came inside.

"Listen, first I'll let you get the half ounce to see how fast you could move it."

"The what? I don't know how much weed that is."

Trigger rubbed his bald head.

"Huh? Did that cat teach you anything?"

"No, all he did was give me small bags of weed and told me to sell them ten dollars each."

Trigger directed Zenobia to the dining room area.

"Come on, let me give you some training."

Zenobia admired the dining room color.

"Wow, you have a sky-blue wall?"

Trigger smiled.

"Yeah, I like different color walls. I like to know for sure I'm in a different room instead of looking at the same colors throughout the house."

Zenobia looked up.

"Oh my, that's a beautiful chandelier."

"A little light work up there to see what I'm doing here in the lab."

Trigger pulled out Zenobia's chair from the dining room table.

"Sit in this chair and learn the basics."

Zenobia sat down and pointed.

"What's that right there?"

Trigger pulled the object closer to them.

"This is a scale and it's important to weigh your goods because you don't want to short yourself. Some cats think they know everything and they eyeball it."

Zenobia scratched her scalp.

"What do you mean by eyeball?"

Trigger grabbed some marijuana and stuffed it in a small bag.

"They do this without weighing it because they trust their eyes to measure. They put just enough in to make a blunt. That's inaccurate though because they give too much or too little of the goods that way. If you put too little you lose out on business because weed heads stay wanting fat bags, and if you put too much you're messing up your profit. Speaking of profit, you better listen to Biggie Ten Crack Commandments song and remember rule number four, never get high on your own supply."

"Wait, because I'm tired of hearing that. I mean, we're not selling crack."

"But majority of the rules still apply."

Zenobia took mental notes.

"Cool, now tell me how to make the ten-dollar bags I used to sell."

Trigger got up and took the digital scale from the china cabinet, then sat next to Zenobia.

"Here, I have extra scales and this one yours to keep."

Zenobia smiled and grabbed the electronic scale.

"Thank you."

"Turn it on and put a half gram of bud on it."

Zenobia grabbed the marijuana and looked down at the scale.

"How would I know if it's right?"

Trigger leaned over towards her.

"You'll see point five here, that's called a dime, which is worth ten dollars."

Zenobia put enough marijuana on the scale until it read point five, then she jumped out her seat.

"I did it!"

Trigger gave Zenobia a small bag.

"Good job, now sit down and put it in here."

Zenobia immediately sat down and put the marijuana in the small bag.

"Done. How many more should I bag up?"

Trigger gave Zenobia a bigger bag.

"Here, make a dub. The scale should say one gram and you'll see one point zero, which is worth twenty dollars."

Zenobia's heart started beating faster.

"Wow, I never sold a big bag like this."

Trigger grabbed a big zip lock bag full of marijuana.

"Listen, I reup by the pounds then I break them down. You're looking at a quarter pound now."

Zenobia placed both hands on top of her dreadlocks.

"Huh? You're losing me."

Trigger laughed.

"My bad, let me slow down because I skipped some information. Some weed heads are smart and they'll ask for eighths. That's three point five on the scale. The eighth is seventy dollars worth of goods and you sell it forty to fifty easy. I sell my eighths for forty to keep them coming back faster."

"Cool."

"Last two for the day. When someone asks you for a water that means quarter and that's seven grams. We'll discuss prices soon. When they say onion, they want the ounce which is twenty-eight grams."

Trigger decided to teach Zenobia how to shoot a gun.

"Come on, we're about to take a trip to PA."

Zenobia stayed in her seat.

"PA? What's going on out there?"

"You need a gun so I'm taking you to Sunset Hill Shooting Range."

Zenobia didn't want to mention she had a .22 because she didn't want Faheem's murder to come up.

"Cool, I never been there. Besides, I need a gun for protection because Shotgun won't be satisfied until I'm dead, with his hating ass."

"True, now come on."

Zenobia stood up and followed Trigger to the car. Once they arrived at the shooting range, Trigger taught Zenobia the correct way to shoot a 12-gauge shotgun, 38 revolver handgun, and a .45 handgun.

"Our shooting session is over."

Zenobia put the .45 down then took her safety glasses and hearing protection off.

"Dag, I was just warming up."

Trigger put his arm across her shoulders.

"Good job. You trained to go and ready for war now."

Zenobia moved Trigger's arm off her.

"Get off me before I catch a body in PA."

They shared a laugh together.

"Stop being silly girl and let's get back to the hood and get this money."

"Just for the record, my last year of school starts next week. Two more semesters and I'll be a college graduate."

Trigger didn't know what to say.

"No worries Boss Man, I'll have this bud game on lock being

that I know all the weed heads at school."

Trigger rubbed his bald head.

"That's what's up. Make sure you get familiar with the biology lab because I'd love to learn some new stuff."

Mary kept threatening Zenobia about getting a job or moving out, so Zenobia was happy about starting the next semester. Staying on campus always felt like Zenobia had her own apartment. Mary never knew about her daughter's illegal hustle. Zenobia figured since most students who attended Rutgers University smoked, that would be the best place to continue hustling.

Selling weed to students on school grounds meant she'd soon be sitting on a goldmine. Living on campus was always a wonderful experience for Zenobia. Being that she was on her own, she did whatever she wanted. She also started missing Sylvia. But she was happy about not getting a new roommate to replace her. Selling marijuana on campus was exciting because on the university grounds, she felt like she was in charge.

Two weeks later Zenobia was nervous about how fast the money started coming, so she called Trigger.

"Hello, are you okay? I'm not used to you calling me this early."

"I need to get this off my chest before class. Honest, I'm not ready for all of that weight at one time."

She heard Trigger turn his music down.

"You shouldn't be in this game if you not ready to get this easy money then, baby girl. Maybe you should reconsider this business because it's dangerous, and that's real coming from a man of my status."

"Thanks for the truth. I'll see you soon."

Zenobia hung the phone up then went to the bathroom to brush her teeth. Afterward, she took a shower and thought about the words that came out Trigger's mouth. *Dag, I can't believe it's been only two weeks and I have a stack of money. I'll continue hustling, but what am I going to do a month or year from now? I need a safe or something to stash this cash because if I put it in the bank, they'll start investigating to figure out where the funds coming from. My B's and C's in all my college courses not bad. However, math and business are my favorite classes, so I'll focus on getting A's there. I need to get the biology club together because I'm tired of them calling me a street pharmacist. I know all types of people talking about me selling weed on campus, but I'm not trying to get caught and kicked out of school. As a matter of fact, I don't care about the name calling because I'm making too much money to let anyone's opinion get to me.*

(Five days later ... Phone rings)

Zenobia didn't recognize the number. Instantly, she dried one hand off to reach for her phone.

"Hello, who is this?"

"Hey sis, it's me Shante. I have a new number. Are you okay? What's that noise?"

"Hold on Shante, you're on speaker phone; let me get out the shower."

"Okay."

"I'm back, drying off now."

"I hear you much better now that you turned the water off. Are you okay?"

Zenobia started putting lotion on her body.

"Yes, I'm maintaining. Why do you sound extra concerned

though? I hope you're okay."

"I have status in the hood just know I stay good. Anyway, some dude by the name of Shotgun approached me in the hood when I visited my Grape homies, talking about I'm going to pay for the problems you caused him. I hope you didn't let him smash. I told him don't come around the way anymore or he's food; trust me. I put that on my C's."

Zenobia put her bra and panties on.

"Girl, when did you start talking that killer stuff like a gangster? I'm still a virgin. Listen, he's not my type at all. I was hustling for him. Shante, please don't tell Mommy either because I'll never hear the end of it."

"Sis stop fuckin' wit' him. I'll holla at one of my homies and get you a Loc deal."

Zenobia left the bathroom after putting her bra on and went to the room to iron her clothes. She placed the phone on the iron board and kept it on speaker.

"I stopped messing with him already, that's why he's mad. I need a new connect though. My supplies getting low because my guy by the name of Trigger got bagged about a week ago."

"Dag, do he have bail money?"

"I didn't hear from him yet so I'm not sure. Anyway, what the hell is a Loc and your Grape homie?

"A Crip, girl. Duh and Grapes are in the same family as Crips. Mommy don't know either because I hide my flag when I'm around her. Well, just like you said to me, please don't tell Mommy I'm a gang member because I'll never hear the end of it, ever."

"All right, your secret is safe with me, and I see this why it took me so long to hear from you because of your new friends. I miss when you had less friends. I know you were into fighting, but I never thought you would have these new friends who are gang members. So, what kind of flag?"

"My blue and white bandana."

Zenobia almost dropped the phone and iron on the floor.

"Oh, I know that gang. They say what's cracking right?" Shante giggled.

"Yeah, that's us and it's craccin' not cracking."

Zenobia put her jeans and shirt on.

"Enough with the Crip knowledge please. Anyway … word … you can really get me the hook up?"

"Word. Being 'dat I'm under his set, my OG Headshot look out for me, but I have to act like it's for me."

"OG? What or who is that?"

"He's da Original Gangsta' who been in da gang for a long time. Everyone respects him and look up to him. He put in that work to get that status. He's a father, boss, and friend all in one."

Zenobia put her socks and sneakers on.

"Okay. Set it up and I'll see you soon. I have to get to class. I love you and stay safe out there."

"Say no more. Save my number Zee, I love you more."

Shante did her part. Zenobia had more weed smokers hooked on her marijuana. One or two puffs had them high to the sky. Their eyes were so low they looked Asian. She felt good knowing she was making people happy all over the world because they made her happy, too well, at least at that moment. She had the bud game on lock. Her business management courses taught her a lot about being a successful boss.

Unfortunately, it all started ending when word got out that Shante was Zenobia's new supplier since Trigger was in police custody. The streets weren't only watching, they were talking, too. The competitors couldn't get to Zenobia, so they got the closest person to her. No, she didn't stop grinding, but she did slow down tremendously. She had a few guns because once she stopped doing business with Shotgun, Zenobia had to watch her back. She had to stay strapped for protection. She was too big and had no time to move around without the steel. Zenobia had to be ready for a shoot-out living the fast life. She knew she would have to face Shotgun again.

Zenobia walked to the corner store on Bergen Street and Avon Avenue with Shante to get a hot pastrami and cheese sandwich. That day burned in her memory. Starving and ready to eat, Zenobia spotted three Bloods getting some dutches and some loosies. So did Shante.

Zenobia whispered.

"Sis, that's them punks who followed me for three blocks on my way to meet you, then they pulled on the side of me at the red light on Clinton Avenue and Bergen Street. Their windows were down so I took a good look at their faces and the red Ford rental truck while they stared as if they wanted to carjack me. I have a bad feeling they do business with Shotgun, and I'm waiting for the truth to come out."

"Listen Zee, we have to play da cut hard because they have something against me, too. I remember them clowns staring me down the day Shotgun approached me about you. One of them bumped me and said my bad, but I knew it was intentional. You're right about them doing business with Shotgun. Now I'm starting to think they're trying to catch us slippin'. Damn, we slippin' right now. Lef' da ratchet in da hood … Dumb move, I know. You too, right? I mean, you lef' your Louie bag in your car. I know you keep the steel there."

Shante rubbed her forehead.

"Dag, you're right!"

The worker at the corner store blew their cover. Poppy screamed out from behind the register.

"Baby cuz, y'all sandwiches ready."

To this day Zenobia believed that Spanish man at the corner store set her and Shante up. At the sound of Poppy's voice, Shante jumped then held her hand on her mouth because she didn't know what to do next, and Zenobia almost defecated on herself. Those Bloods turned around so fast. Before they knew it the three gangsters were on their behinds, ready to hurt them. The sisters thought they were going to die until seconds after they both began swinging. They then realized the Blood gang members didn't have guns either. Shante managed to get her Snapple bottle that she purchased with her sandwich and busted the biggest dude on his head with it. Then she started running. Zenobia was right behind her.

"Hurry up girl before more of them come."

"Keep running, I'm right behind you. Dag, where your homies at when we need them?"

"They're out here. Hold on though because I'm out of breath."

By the time they ran to Crazyville (Bergen Street Townhouses), Shante felt weak and dizzy. Her Grape homies came over to her yelling.

"Yo, cuz, what happened?"

Zenobia was out of breath, trying to breathe and speak at the same time. She struggled with her words. "Them … them—"

Shante interrupted.

"Them Slob niggahs jumped us."

Shante's Crip gang member Crunk Loc grabbed Shante to prevent her from falling. He felt something wet.

"Yo cuz, niggas poked you up."

Zenobia looked down and noticed blood all over Shante's gray T-shirt.

Shante spoke her last words before fainting.

"Damn, 'dem niggahs milked me!"

Instantly Zenobia realized one of those guys by that corner store stabbed Shante, so she ran across the street to get her car. Once she got back to Shante, Zenobia and Crunk Loc picked her up, put her in the car, and rushed her to UMD, the nearest hospital.

Every day Zenobia was at the hospital praying for a speedy recovery. Three days later, Shante woke up from the coma. Zenobia wanted to communicate with her.

"Sis, are you all right? Sis, can you hear me? Are you okay?"

Shante's eyes were half opened. For sure she recognized Zenobia's voice. She tried to jump up, but the IV and bandages kept her from moving so fast. Shante opened her mouth to speak, but her throat was too dry. Shante's heart monitor started beeping so the nurse on duty at the time came in and informed Zenobia to leave the hospital room.

"I'm sorry, I have to ask you to leave the room because you're upsetting my patient."

Zenobia looked down at the nurse's name tag.

"Nurse Faison, your patient is my sister and she's excited to see me. Can you please let me stay here with her, please? I refuse to leave her side."

Zenobia felt as if she was begging for her own life as well. It worked because she didn't have to leave. Nurse Faison gave Shante some water and examined her.

"Shante, do you remember anything that happened to you?"

Shante responded weakly.

"No, I don't rememba' anything at all. Can you please tell me?"

Without a doubt, the look in Shante's eyes told Zenobia differently. She knew Shante had remembered exactly what happened.

Nurse Faison proceeded to share her part of the story, which Zenobia had told the staff the first day they arrived at the hospital.

"Some guys tried to rob you and left you for dead, but your sister found you and got you here just in time, young lady."

In and out of consciousness, Shante knew that was just a cover up. Zenobia was always on point, especially when it came to keeping the cops off their behinds. Also, Zenobia didn't need the cops involved with the retaliation and repercussions they had for them Bloods.

The day Shante was released from the hospital, Dr. Brown told her to get some rest so she could heal properly. He must have been on dust or some type of drug because Zenobia and Shante were out there ready for war. Shante wasted no time calling a meeting to chop it up with the 'Locs.'

Once they arrived at Mary's spot, Shante rushed for the house phone.

"What's craccin, cuz? 'Dem Lil Bricks (Felix Fuld Court) niggahs is done … It's a wrap, doobies and pins … I'm 'bout to pop some corns, so plan is definitely in motion, big homie."

When Shante got off the phone Zenobia hugged her.

"No matter what happens tonight, I love you, Shante."

Shante smiled.

"I love you more, sis. Now cut it out like glue in your hair."

About 8:30 PM Shante kept staring at the clock. Her big homie Crunk Loc was supposed to be there like forty-five minutes ago.

"Shante, why don't you stop looking at the time and just call your big homie, ask him how far he is?"

Shante started pacing the floor.

"I can't hit his telly because it was made clear during the trey-sixty: we agreed no discussions over the jack just in case one of us get bagged. The boys would investigate and put two and two together, then everybody goin' down."

"Huh, what's a trey-sixty?"

Shante stopped pacing the floor and brought Zenobia up to date with the details.

"I stay schooling you. It's a meeting with the Crip homies. Real talk, I'm pissed off because I have a feeling big homie Crunk Loc popped an E pill or somethin'. He's only late when he's high. He better never sell pills because he'll stay high off his own supply."

"Hold that thought because my phone at five percent."

As soon as Zenobia headed to the door to get her cell phone charger, one of Shante's gang member friends called Shante on the house phone. She put the call on speaker phone.

"Hello."

"Cuz, come out right now. Don't ask questions."

"Sis, not sure where Big Homie at. Plan still in motion. I'm feeling some type of way though because that was Tune, he always want to be in control of something, let's go."

Instantly, they turned off the lights, ran out of the house, and jumped into a rental truck. The Crips were masked up. Shante put on her mask, and Zenobia followed suit. Tune drove to Little Bricks, and as soon as Tune rolled down all the windows, everyone else started shooting nonstop. Tune circled the block twice. The second time he went around the block, he stopped and got out of the rental truck.

"Get out an' make sho' y'all popped one of 'em."

Zenobia had trust issues, so once Shante got out, she got out too, but an unpleasant feeling sat in the pit of her stomach.

"Shante, your homeboy bugging. We just did a drive-by right here, so why are we still here?"

"Real talk, I'm confused. I really hope Crunk Loc get here soon."

Zenobia had tears in her eyes.

"Sis, I know for a fact something is not right. Please, we need to go. This rental looks real familiar."

Shante looked at the rental.

"Everyone renting them, so it's a lot of them floating around."

Shante put both hands up as she looked to the sky and screamed.

"What da fuck! Tune, what da hell ya doin', punk? You tryin' to get us bodied?"

Suddenly, Blood gang members raced toward them, shooting at the same time. Shante and Zenobia ran toward Crazyville. Out of breath as they were running, Zenobia spoke from her heart.

"I told you this was a set up. I knew it, I remember now."

"What are you talking about? 'Member what, Zenobia?"

"That's them clowns who I told you about from the corner store who followed me on my way to meet you. I remember that same exact Ford truck. Next time you must communicate over the phone. For sure, I think your so-called homie Tune set us up!"

Once they reached Crazyville, Shante started yelling.

"Aay Loc!"

Unfortunately, nobody was outside. They continued to run toward Winans Avenue. That's when they spotted Tune coming down the block in the red Ford rental truck. Shante ran toward the truck and tried to flag him down. Unfortunately, that sucker sped up. Zenobia screamed.

"Sis, get out of the way! I knew it, he's a fraud. Move, he's not going to stop." *Oh my God, it's too late*, she thought.

Shante was out of breath from running, and she couldn't react fast enough. Tune drove straight into her. Shante screamed and fell hard to the ground near a parked car.

"Ahhhh."

Tune drove in reverse, made sure he hit Shante again, and he hit the parked car next to her.

Shante screamed even louder.

"Ahhhh."

What Zenobia witnessed next blew her away. It was unheard of. Two of the "Slobs," as Shante called them from the corner store about a week ago, were in the car with Tune. The guy in the passenger side rolled his window down and teased,

"Yeah, got ya brab ass now, muthafucka."

The other guy in the backseat on the passenger side made his presence known.

"Now you can res' wit' 'dat fag ass nigga, Crunk brab."

Zenobia couldn't believe her two eyes. Not only was Tune a transformer, but Shotgun was in on the setup, too. Shotgun chuckled as he got out of the rental truck and pointed his gun to Zenobia's forehead.

"You thought I was gonna let you go 'dat easy, bitch? You betta leave my streets, if not I'ma kill you."

Zenobia cried and hugged Shante.

"I love you. Tell everyone else I love them, too."

"I love you too, but if this niggah kill you, I swear to God he betta' kill me too."

Shante and Zenobia finally understood why her big homie Crunk Loc never showed up at the house. He was already dead. At that moment, Zenobia sincerely believed with all her heart that God is real. Shotgun didn't have the heart to murder her or Shante. Once they pulled off, police sirens grew near, headed toward their direction. Zenobia had difficulty breathing and her heart started racing.

"Shante, we have to go. My chest starting to hurt."

Shante strained with all her might.

"I can't … I can't move …"

Shante couldn't move her legs because they were stuck between the sidewalk and the front tire of a parked car. They knew instantly her legs were broken. Zenobia flagged down a taxi driver since her car was parked too far away. She didn't want to take any more chances. She was unable to contact Mary because her battery was dead.

Shante was back at UMD Hospital. Zenobia couldn't stop praying because it was just like déjà vu all over again. It felt exactly like last week when Shante got stabbed at that corner store. The only difference was that she had to stay longer because she was paralyzed from the waist down. Shante would be in a wheelchair for the rest of her life. Zenobia felt miserably guilty.

One day when Zenobia went to check up on Shante, she hesitated to go inside her hospital room because she heard her talking to her OG Headshot. Before Zenobia entered, she eavesdropped because she was a little afraid of facing him. She'd never met him because Shante had to pretend like the marijuana she got from him was for her.

"What's up, OG? I must keep it real wit' you 'cause I don't know if I'm gonna make it much longer."

"Okay, stop wit' 'dat not gonna make it shit! What's goin' on, loccette?"

Shante struggled, pulling her head up on the pillow.

"When I was coppin' off you, 'dat wasn't my work. It was for my oldest sis. She's da hustla'. I don't sell Cali. Hustle is in her DNA. She was jus' hittin' me off lovely 'cause you gave her a certified Loc deal."

OG Headshot stood up from the chair by the hospital bed and held the pillow for her.

"Thanks for keepin' it real wit' me. I knew it was for her and not you. The money was always good, so I didn't say anything. Jus' for 'dat, I'm still gonna be yo' sis connect, if she still want to get dis money, shorty loc."

"Dat's what's craccin'. She'll be here soon, so y'all can politic then …"

Shante laughed out loud as she noticed a shadow outside the door.

"Now you can come inside and stop ear hustlin', sis."

Finally, Zenobia got the courage to enter Shante's room. Her heart was beating so fast. She just knew OG Headshot was going to murder her. Zenobia tried to fit in and feel safe. She started sounding like a Crip since their language grew on her

"What's craccin', cuz?"

"Kicc cacc coolin'. Have a seat here. So, I heard ya big time on da streets thanks to me."

Zenobia sat down and pointed at Shante.

"Yes, that's true, thanks to my little sister right there."

"So, do you wanna keep doin' ya numbas?"

"I'm not trying to be smart, but America is a money-making world. It's money out there to get. Honest, I'm going to get it. I'm not greedy, I just want a slice of the pie."

"Say no more, youngin', I got you. Let me get out of here. I'll get your number from her and holla at y'all later. C Easy, Cuz."

OG Headshot gave Shante a Crip handshake then left the hospital room. Zenobia just watched.

"That was an interesting handshake."

"Yeah, I had to study that. It took me a minute to learn."

"I bet."

"Do you want me to teach you?"

"No, it was interesting to see though."

Zenobia talked to Shante and watched television with her until she fell asleep. Zenobia stayed and wrote a poem before she left because she hated seeing her sister in that predicament.

That was the past and beginning of Zenobia's misery.

Dear Diary,

POEM

Guilty

Instead of getting a new connect I should have let the fast life rest

Now the haters coming for my head and neck

Getting money was always my favorite dialect

Sometimes I wish I could hide in someone's attic

When I witnessed Shante get stabbed and hit by that rental truck it almost caused me to have a heart attack

CHAPTER NINE

Warning Shot

One month later, Zenobia decided to have some wine to clear her mind. Just before she reached the 43rd Street Café Lounge, she noticed a Lincoln town car behind her with the headlights off. *Oh, hell no! Is this car following me?* She didn't want to cause any attention to herself, so she drove around the same block twice just to be certain the car in the rearview was really following her and it wasn't coincidental. Her .45 pistol was absent, but she knew she needed to be cautious being that it was dark. Once she got back on Springfield Avenue, she made a left on Lyons Avenue and a right on Wilson Place. Sadly, the streetlights didn't work on Wilson Place, which made the situation scarier. Zenobia should have had some type of protection, but at that moment she wasn't thinking. When the vehicle cornered her on Wilson Place, she just knew it was the end of her life.

Zenobia rolled her window down.

"What's good? Do I know one of you?"

The driver got out the car and pointed his .9-millimeter Glock in her face. He took his hoody off.

"You know what time it is, dog. Get down or lay down."

Zenobia's heart felt like it slipped into her feet as her forehead started to wrinkle. The driver kept waving the gun in her direction. His jaw twitched. She gripped the steering wheel with one hand and squeezed the seatbelt with her other hand because she didn't know when the short guy was going to squeeze the trigger.

"Listen, I think it's some type of misunderstanding because I'm human, I'm not your dog."

The driver almost broke the door handle.

"Bitch stop bein' funny. Open the door an' give me yo' Kia because this shit mine now."

Tears slid down to Zenobia's shirt as she exited the car. Simultaneously, the dude in the passenger seat threatened Zenobia and took all her money.

"Empty yo' pockets an' yo' bra before I blast yo' ugly ass. Yeah, I know bitches hide money in dem thangs"

Once they succeeded in robbing her for her possessions, the driver told the passenger to get his belongings.

"Dog, get my charger out 'dat shit an' let's get da fuck outta here. Dis G ride fire. I didn't know Kia's come fully loaded like this."

A silent relief came over Zenobia. To her surprise, it got worse. Another car arrived and four dudes stumbled out that vehicle. They were going back and forth trying to take the car from the two guys who had just stolen it from her.

"Yo, what y'all two doing in our territory?"

"We have beef with her."

"It's with us now 'cause dis our hood."

Their speech was slurred, but once the guy in charge shot one bullet in the sky, the arguing, yelling, and screaming at each other stopped. Zenobia looked around and planned her escape. Petrified, she couldn't believe all of this had happened so quickly. She knew she was in the wrong place at the wrong time, or so she thought. Finally, she had the opportunity to get away since everyone else was focused on the shooter to make sure he didn't pull the trigger again. Zenobia took off running. As soon as she ran to the corner, she heard the passenger shout "Son, fuck 'dat car and these four. They can keep this shit because it's a push start, so they can't get far without her remote. C'mon, Shorty tryna get away. Get her before it's too late."

Three gunshots rang loud in Zenobia's ears. She ran faster, but unfortunately, a fourth shot was fired, and it caught her in the leg. Instantly she screamed then dropped to the ground. She attempted to get back up, but she fell again. Afterward she held her leg.

"What do you two want with my life? Here's the remote to my car, I won't report it stolen. Please don't kill me. I'm begging you, don't kill me." *I need to get out this mess because I can't die like this*, she thought.

The passenger stood over Zenobia, shaking the gun by her bloody leg.

"You betta stop hustlin' or else, 'cause I'm tired of competin' wit' you. An' 'dat was a warnin' shot, so don't try me because I'm not Shotgun. I will shoot. Dat's why he sent me this time, and if he send me again, yo' ass is grass. Know 'dat."

Annoyed, frustrated, and in pain, Zenobia used her shirt to wipe the tears.

Unbelievable! Shotgun had set me up again. Well, I'm still happy they let me live.

It all came together that night. It was easy shooting someone with a gun. Consequently, it was painful taking a bullet. That warning shot shattered Zenobia's leg and she had to depend on crutches for a couple months. She collected the last of her money then realized she had to put an end to living the fast life. Truthfully, she knew she had plenty of chances to stop, but she became greedy. That night she went home and had a talk with her higher power.

God, I know you told me to stop when Shante became paralyzed, but I didn't listen. Well, thank you so much for sparing my life. It's a blessing to still be alive. I had too many wake up calls. Honest, I understand I might not get another chance. Therefore, I hear you loud and clear now. I'm leaving the drug game alone and instead I'ma get a man, so I can have a baby. I know Mommy waiting for a grandchild. Amen.

Zenobia tried to calm that worried feeling in her stomach. She wasted no time calling OG Headshot.

"Hello … Hello, do you hear me?"

OG Headshot sounded like he just woke up.

"What's going on wit' cha? About time you decided to call me, you had me stressing. I been sleeping a lot, like I got a chick pregnant or something."

"Listen, OG, I'm done with this lifestyle because it's too risky and stressful."

Zenobia heard OG Headshot throw an object against the wall, which caused her to almost drop the phone.

"Check dis out. Business is slow wit' out cha. You been going harder than the dudes. I'm willing to drop the prices for you. I'll give you a pound for seventeen hundred."

Zenobia was hesitant because she thought about the bigger profit.

"No … deal."

"Okay, sixteen fifty."

Zenobia was still a little delayed with her response.

"No … deal."

Zenobia heard OG Headshot slam his door

"Okay. Dis my final offer—sixteen hundred and nothin' lower. I hope you don't think you're getting it for free."

Zenobia left the living room full of confidence to sit outside on the porch.

"No deal! No thank you. I'm over that life because it's too dangerous. Not only did it cause me to get shot, but they got my sister, too and she's in a wheelchair for the rest of her life. I'd rather work for minimum wage."

"Yo, you knew what it was when you got in dis biz'ness."

Zenobia started walking, she was getting ready to hang up.

"At the time I didn't care. Real talk, I'm wiser now and the streets not worth it at all. You know and I know: 'live by the gun die by the gun.' I will not change my mind either; so, do not ask me again. No amount of money is worth my freedom or life because if I'm in the penitentiary or dead, I won't be able to spend it."

"Fuck you. An' you betta neva need me fo' shit!"

"I'm tired of listening to you scream in my ear. I promise I'll never need you and I'm deleting your number."

Zenobia started evaluating her life then wrote her feelings down before she went to bed.

Dear Diary,

I'm not proud of my two-point five grade-point average, but I'm happy I accomplished my educational goals. Damn sperm donor didn't show up for my college graduation. I bet when he dies, I won't even be named in his obituary as his daughter either, and that's fine because I'm finally at peace with myself. I did my best to try to get to know him. Some people will always assume, while I know the facts.

Finally, I'm moving forward with my life. Everything happens for a reason. I used to feel bad about not having my dad in my life, but no more looking back because I'm not going in that direction. My mother is the best and she helped me to appreciate the family I have. Instead of focusing on who's not in my life, I'm grateful for Mary, Shante, Rose, and Pudge. Don't get me wrong because sometimes I still hurt. I'm healing though, and I refuse to stress because life goes on.

CHAPTER TEN

Storm

The life of a hustler wasn't all it was cracked up to be. Not only was it dangerous, but it took up too much of Zenobia's time. She had no type of social life. She never had a moment for anything or anyone, except marijuana and the smokers. Either she was busy getting money, or busy figuring out how to get more money. It began to take a toll on her. She became overly emotional. She was curious about sex so when she finally stopped hustling she wanted someone to connect with. In her search for someone who would love her flaws and see past her mistakes, she found herself looking for love in all the wrong places.

Sex became her quick moment of attachment. She went from being addicted to the fast life to becoming addicted to sex. When Zenobia was in the arms of multiple men, she felt wanted, needed, and accepted. A part of her knew she was fooling herself. She knew none of those men really cared about her, but in her imaginary world she was in control. The truth is, Zenobia wasn't in control at all. In fact, she was completely out of control. She was promiscuous with so many men that each time she became pregnant she got an abortion because she never knew who the father was. Zenobia couldn't fathom her child asking about his or her father and not having a clue as to who he really was. She knew what it was like growing up without a father, so she didn't want her child to go through the same thing.

Having abortions never got easier. Zenobia always felt so nervous and alone, especially in the waiting area with all sorts of thoughts racing through her head. No one ever went to the abortion clinic with her because she never told Mary or anyone else that she was pregnant.

"Zenobia Jordan, come with me."

Zenobia followed nurse Culver into the room. Once she entered the room, nurse Culver questioned her.

"Are you by yourself?"

"No, well, yes, but do I need someone with me?"

"It's up to you. However, since you're by yourself you'll have to stay awake during the process. Are you fine with that?"

"Okay, I guess."

Nurse Culver handed Zenobia two gowns.

"Take off your clothes and put one gown in the front and the other in the back, then wait for Dr. Moore."

"Hello, my name is Dr. Moore. Did nurse Culver go over the procedure?"

"A little."

"For starters, I can't give you anesthesia because you don't have anyone with you to make sure you get home safely once you wake up."

Zenobia sat in the chair by the door.

"I understand … I'm going to fill every bit of the pain, right?"

"No, I'm going to numb you from the waist down, therefore, you'll be all right. Let me go over your medical history."

"Sure."

Afterward Zenobia was given a brief physical examination that determined when pregnancy began and was checked for sexually transmitted diseases. Also, Dr. Moore had to make sure Zenobia was healthy enough to undergo the procedure. Dr. Moore directed Zenobia to the operating room.

"Zenobia let's go to the other room and get this done for you."

Zenobia hesitated before she went in. She stood in the doorway and scanned the room.

"Please don't hurt me, Doc' this is my first time being pregnant."

Dr. Moore pointed to the operating area.

"Come in and relax."

Zenobia positioned herself on her stomach. Dr. Moore washed his hands and put his gloves on.

"Turn on your back. Here we go young lady. One … Two … Three …"

Zenobia closed her eyes.

"Ouch!"

Zenobia screamed louder as she opened her eyes.

"You lied and said I'll be all right. BULLSHIT! That junk hurt."

Pain and discomfort showed on Zenobia's face. Not only was it emotionally painful because she was about to kill a human and stop a beating heart, but it was physically painful, too. Zenobia literally felt every inch of that needle he stuck inside her. The procedure was known as a surgical abortion, or suction aspiration, and it was during her first trimester.

The syringe used was a vacuum-type instrument that was placed into her vagina. Dr. Moore claimed she would only feel a cramping type feeling. Oh God! He lied! That vacuum not only sucked the baby out of her, surprisingly it felt like it was taking every piece of her organs out. The noise from the vacuum was so loud it drained out her thoughts. She then zoned out. Once the abortion was done, she signed release papers and got her prescription for pain medicine. Afterward, Zenobia called a taxicab and went to Rite Aid in Irvington Center on Springfield Avenue to get her prescription filled. Next, she walked to the Gallery Holiday Motel on

Ball Street.

Once she arrived, she used an alias. For four days straight, Zenobia slept and didn't eat or wash. She turned her cellular phone off and decided if she wanted to take the pain pills or sleep the pain away.

Although she was ashamed to admit it, she went through the same procedure six different times. After each abortion she was traumatized. She felt so bad and wished she had never had any at all. Each time Zenobia went to the clinic, it was like being out of touch with herself … her real self. It felt as if pieces of her heart were being ripped out. Still she couldn't believe she had gone through the same course of action repeatedly. Every year thoughts of how old her children would have been haunted her and it hurt her to her soul. She became that girl she said she would never be. Zenobia allowed men to use her body as their playground and in return, she was hoping to feel loved. Yet, all she ended up with was morning sickness and regular trips to the abortion clinic. During the sixth abortion, Zenobia decided she wouldn't terminate her next pregnancy. Part of her felt like it would stop the feelings of guilt. She also decided to commit to one man and have at least one baby to forgive herself for all the abortions she had in the past.

One day Zenobia went to Weequahic Park to clear her mind and she noticed a gentleman sitting on the bench staring at her.

"Hello, you're too pretty to walk this trail by yourself. Can I join you?"

Zenobia blushed.

"Hello, thank you so much for the kind words. I'll be a fool to say no, so come on."

The gentleman stood up, happy like a little child in the candy store. Then he went down to a running form.

"On your mark, get set, go!"

Zenobia looked down at him with her eyebrows raised.

"Are you serious, because my running days been over."

The gentleman stood up.

"Sike, nah I'm just having fun with you."

They shared a laugh together.

"What's your name?"

"My name is Lamar. I bet your name is Pretty."

Zenobia blushed harder than before.

"Do you write, because I'm feeling your wordplay?"

"I used to ghostwrite for a few people."

"Good to know. Well, I write a little poetry in my diary so let's meet on the other side of the park tomorrow at twelve noon. Oh, my name is Zee, short for Zenobia."

Lamar turned in a circle and pointed to sections of the park.

"Zee, you know Weequahic Park is at least three hundred acres, now exactly where do you want to meet at?"

Zenobia pointed.

"Over there by the monkey bars, where the guys working out at."

Lamar followed Zenobia's finger.

"Bet, see you over there at noon, and don't have me waiting too long."

Zenobia thought Lamar was the perfect gentleman. He favored Tyrese Gibson, but with waves. Respectful, well-mannered, he treated her amazing, so she just knew he would be a great father. Lamar was always so concerned about her. He protected and provided for her. Most importantly, he made Zenobia feel like the queen she deserved to be treated like. Every morning he called just to say good morning, and if she was still asleep, he left a good morning voicemail and text message. Also, Lamar called every night just to say good night, and if she was asleep, he left a good night voicemail and text message. Zenobia assumed he was her soul mate, so she moved in with him after dating for only three months.

Unfortunately, she was wrong with her assumption. One month later it all changed when he got fired from his job. She couldn't recall the first time he hit her because they fought often. Her prince charming went from protecting her to controlling her. Zenobia felt like a peasant instead of a queen. Like an abused, helpless character in a Lifetime movie, she couldn't believe how her life had taken a turn for the worse. Lamar beat her if she walked too loudly, smiled too hard, or even took a shower too long. He made her feel as if she deserved every slap, punch, and kick he delivered. Jada, the downstairs neighbor, started getting concerned.

"Zee, I was waiting for you to come down here to check the mail. How are you?"

Zenobia unlocked the mailbox.

"I'm good. How are you?"

Jada folded her arms.

"Girl, you don't have to lie to me. I always hear you and Lamar arguing."

Zenobia took the mail out and locked the mailbox.

"We have our ups and downs, but we'll be all right."

Jada opened the door wider.

"Come inside so we can talk without your man hearing us."

Zenobia separated her mail from Lamar's.

"We can chat right here."

Jada took a deep breath.

"Why don't you call the cops or leave this unhealthy relationship?"

Zenobia looked up the stairs to make sure Lamar wasn't listening.

"Well, he was my light when I was in the darkest place of my life, and he was the only man who ever stuck around me. Also, I want to have a child with him because the baby would make our relationship better."

"I don't know who need help more, you or him, because this is beyond scary. Can't you see he's not trying to get another job because his controlling manipulative behind is satisfied living off you?"

Lamar came down the stairs.

"What's taking you so long to get the mail?"

Zenobia almost dropped the mail.

"Trying to tell Jada we're okay and she don't have to call the cops."

Lamar stormed towards Jada and she slammed the door in his face.

"You better hide behind that door, mind your fucking business! Ha-ha that's why you don't got a man now."

Jada responded behind her closed door.

"Actually, I don't have a man because I know my worth and I'm taking care of me first."

Lamar punched Jada's door.

"Whatever goes on in my house stays in my house. You better never call the cops on us."

Jada kicked the door from the inside.

"I don't have any respect for you Lamar, and I'm praying for Zee. Oh, you can always call me if you need to vent."

Lamar looked at Zenobia and pointed upstairs.

"Get your ass in the house, and I better not ever catch you talking to that miserable piece of shit again."

Zenobia loved Lamar with everything she had left. She pretended they had the best relationship. She worshiped the ground he walked on. Sad to say, she loved him more than she loved herself. She knew she couldn't call the police on him and watch him go through a felony charge for assault. Although it's disheartening to reveal, she took the beatings like a man, and in some strange way she felt it was worth it. Zenobia wished and prayed that Lamar's abusive ways would stop. She hid the truth—her pride wouldn't let her tell anyone her business.

One afternoon she and Lamar were in the bedroom watching the ID Channel. *Fatal Vows* was on. Particularly, Season 2, Episode 3, "Romance Reloaded" gave Zenobia the courage to speak to Lamar about his behavior.

"Babe, maybe you should consider getting evaluated. You might be mentally ill, or maybe you have a case of bipolar disorder."

"Bipolar my ass, stop playing with me."

Zenobia turned the television off.

"I mean you go from cold to hot within seconds, and it's scary. I'm really getting concerned, so I think you should get some help … maybe get admitted to the nearest psychiatric hospital."

Lamar slapped Zenobia on her face instantly; she held her face as a tear fell.

"Before our relationship ends, Lamar, I can't keep letting you hit on me like this. You're going to kill me."

Lamar choked Zenobia. She tried reaching for the remote control to hit him in the face with it. He gripped harder on her neck then tossed the pillows and remote on the floor.

"I told you to stop playing with me. I'm not bipolar, you just make me go from zero to a hunnit real quick."

Zenobia started yelling and screaming.

"I'll even go to counseling with you to see a therapist … or psychiatrist … or anger management counselor. Whatever you decide."

Lamar's dark skin turned red as he dragged Zenobia into the living room.

"I'm tired of repeating myself."

Sadly, that evening they got into their regular combats, but this time was different. Before she could utter another word, he pulled her up on the black fluffy couch. Then Lamar's closed fist met Zenobia's face and knocked her out.

"You better learn to listen to me because I am God. Do I make my fuckin' self clear?"

Zenobia fell onto the floor, unconscious. Lamar kept walking from her head to her feet, hitting himself in the head.

"Fuck my life! I hope I didn't kill this hardheaded bitch."

Lamar felt a weak pulse.

"Good, she's still alive, let me get her keys and drive her to the hospital. Damn where her keys at? Fuck it, I'll just call the ambulance."

All Zenobia remembered was waking up the next day in a Beth Israel hospital room with a broken nose. Lamar stood at her bedside as Zenobia opened her eyes. She wasn't ready to look at Lamar, so she put the sheet over her face. Lamar looked down at her and whispered.

"I'm sorry—I called the ambulance last night. I didn't mean to hit you that hard."

Zenobia knew this might sound a little crazy to an outsider, but Lamar was by her side when she felt worthless, therefore, she didn't want to give up on him.

"Please stop covering your face and look at me because I'm sorry."

Zenobia pulled the sheet below her eyes. Lamar leaned over her. Zenobia jumped with fear in her eyes.

"What are you doing?"

Zenobia pulled the sheet over her face again. Lamar sat on the chair next to the bed.

"I was going to kiss you on your forehead. You don't have to be afraid of me."

Zenobia pulled the sheet to her waist and sat up on the bed.

"Look what you did to me. How do you expect me not to be afraid?"

Lamar pulled the chair closer to the bed.

"I'm begging you not to tell anyone, and I promise I would never hit you again … I'm sorry"

Zenobia closed her eyes for a moment then opened them.

"I believe you because you said sorry more than once, and you're right here with me."

"Good morning, Ms. Jordan, I'm Officer Johnson and she's Officer Giddens. I'm not going to sugar coat this, tell me about these injuries you sustained."

Zenobia lightly rubbed her nose twice because it pained her as she spoke.

"I fell."

Both officers looked at each other, then Officer Giddens tried talking to Zenobia woman to woman.

"Zenobia, domestic violence isn't love. I was in an abusive relationship about seven years ago, that's why I decided to become a domestic violence prevention police officer. I love being on the Domestic Violence Response Team because it's an amazing feeling when I help people like you. Can you tell me the truth about your broken nose?"

Zenobia started crying.

"With all due respect Officer, I'm not you. My nose is throbbing, so I need to sleep away this pain. I fell is my final answer."

Officer Giddens didn't believe Zenobia, but she had to accept her answer being that she had no witnesses.

"Here's my card if you ever need to talk. Never be afraid to get help and make the right decisions."

Zenobia didn't want to take the business card, but she took it because she wanted Officers Johnson and Giddens to leave her hospital room.

"Thank you, I guess."

One month later, Zenobia joined a boxing gym because she needed to learn the correct way to defend herself. Her intuition told her Lamar may hit her again if she didn't find a way to convince him to get professional help. Zenobia wrote the name 'Lamar' on a piece of paper and taped it to the heavy bag. Every time she punched the bag it felt as if she was hitting Lamar. It was so much fun punching the heavy bag and speed bag. Her boxing coach, Apollo Kidd, was the best trainer and boxer. She'd recommend him to anyone because his boxing record spoke for itself. It was difficult for him to get fighting matches because most of his opponents didn't want to accept the challenge.

Although Lamar claimed he wasn't going to hit Zenobia again, about two months later he did. They were sitting on the loveseat watching *Love & Basketball* in the living room. Lamar had picked up the habit of drinking Coors Light beer.

"Since when did you become a drinker?"

Lamar drank one can of beer then opened a second can.

"I started today, and I enjoy the buzz I get. I don't plan on stopping either."

(Cellular phone rings)

Lamar looked at the name and grabbed Zenobia's phone fast.

"Yo, who is Jay and why is he calling you?"

Zenobia paused the movie and held the remote in her hand as she tried to figure out the guy calling her.

"Who? Let me see my phone."

Lamar put Zenobia's phone close to her face to let her read the name.

"See, who the fuck is Jay?"

Zenobia laughed.

"Boy stop playing. You know that's our neighbor downstairs, Jada. Give me my phone now so I can talk to her."

Lamar stood up and put Zenobia's phone in his army fatigue cargo pants pocket.

"Fuck no, you not about to disrespect me and talk to this dude in front of my face."

Zenobia tried to take her phone out of Lamar's pocket.

"It's Jada. Why don't you believe me?"

Lamar pushed Zenobia's hand away.

"Don't ever try to go in my pocket. I don't trust you because I noticed you been going out five days a week since last month."

Zenobia frowned.

"Are you serious? I've been going to work and to the gym."

"Don't get smart with me. When we met you used to always want to spend time with me. I have proof you're cheating because your time is spent somewhere else."

Zenobia wanted her phone, so she stood up and tried to go in Lamar's pocket again.

"Give me my phone so I can call Jada back."

Lamar smirked, which caught Zenobia off guard. Meanwhile, she couldn't protect herself when he punched her multiple times in the face. Afterward he kicked her in the face and threw her phone on the loveseat.

Zenobia started screaming.

"Go ahead and finish what you started, just kill me!"

Zenobia fell in a fetal position on the loveseat as Lamar stood over her.

"I just thought about it, you been sneaking behind my back and talking to Jada. I guess she got you going to the gym and next she's going to make you think you can whoop my ass, right? For the last time, stop talking to that miserable piece of shit."

Lamar walked away to get another can of beer out the refrigerator. He then walked back to Zenobia.

"Do I make my fuckin' self clear? Why are you ignoring me? You know I hate being ignored."

Zenobia sat up to feel her face since it was throbbing. Instantly, she reached over for her phone to get a better look at herself. Her tears came down faster.

"I hate you! Look what you did."

Lamar noticed Zenobia's jaw swelling up. He took a big gulp of his beer then placed the can on the cherry red hardwood floor. Next, he dragged her off the loveseat and down the stairs. Finally, he banged on Jada's door. Jada was about to bake a lemon cake with vanilla frosting, but she thought it was Zenobia banging on the door. She decided to put the cake pan on the table and turned the oven off.

"I'm coming, I was in the kitchen."

Jada froze when she opened the door, then she snapped out of the daze.

"Why are you banging on my door? I see you forgot you told me to mind my business."

"Shut up and call 9-1-1."

"Call 9-1-1 for what? Remember you threatened me not to call the cops?"

Lamar pointed down.

"Call them and don't tell them I did it."

Jada looked down and screamed.

"Oh no, what did you do to her?"

Lamar pinched his chin twice.

"If you don't hurry and call them, she may die."

Jada closed the door and ran to her phone in the kitchen then dialed 9-1-1.

The dispatcher answered on the first ring.

"9-1-1, what's your emergency?"

Jada kept stuttering.

"M-My-My …"

"Ma'am, can you calm down and tell me your emergency?"

Jada almost knocked the cake pan on the floor as she took a seat at the kitchen table.

"My upstairs neighbor needs medical treatment because her

mouth is swollen and bleeding."

"Okay, help is on the way. Do you know what happened and where is she now?"

Jada went to the bathroom to put some water on her face.

"Um, not really and she's on the floor in the hall."

"Are you sure you didn't do this?"

Jada started walking to the front door.

"No, I'm more than sure I know who did it. I'll put him on the phone before this fall on me."

Jada opened the door and handed the phone to Lamar.

"The dispatcher wants to talk to you."

Lamar hung the phone up.

"I don't have shit to say to them, just make sure she gets to the hospital and pretend I'm not home."

Lamar slammed the door and walked upstairs.

Zenobia couldn't open her mouth because she had limited movement of her jaw, which made it difficult to talk.

"Thank you so much. Please don't tell the police because it was my fault. I should have told you don't call me anymore."

Jada sat on the floor next to Zenobia.

"Stop talking like that because it's not your fault. I'll let the police know your man did this to you."

Zenobia grabbed Jada's leg.

"No, let me handle my own business."

Jada pulled her leg away.

"Okay, I'm convinced I can't save you because you don't want help. I'll leave the front door open, but I'm locking my door. Please don't bother me or I'm reporting Lamar. I'll continue to pray for you though."

Moments later the police arrived and noticed the front door ajar.

"Ma'am, good to see your eyes opened. The paramedics are less than five minutes away. What happened?"

Zenobia held her hand over her mouth.

"I can't talk much; I fell down the stairs."

The officer bent down.

"Are you sure you didn't get pushed down the stairs?"

Zenobia shook her head as the officer made room for EMT.

"Okay, let me get out their way."

EMT noticed Zenobia's swollen and bloody face so they put her in the back of the ambulance, asked some questions, and checked Zenobia's blood pressure as the driver headed to the hospital.

"Hello, I'm shocked to see you at this hospital again. I gave you my business card. Why didn't you call me? Are you going to tell me what happened this time? Please don't say you fell."

Zenobia was shocked to see Officer Giddens and she couldn't believe she had landed back in Beth Israel again. She felt the bandages around her face, from her head to her chin. Instantly, she realized her jaw was broken and she had to eat from a straw.

"A few people jumped me. Oh, um, I didn't see their faces. I don't have anything else to say about it. Please stop with the questions and leave because I don't want to press charges, if that's your next question."

Officer Giddens placed her business card on the chair and walked away.

"That's another one of my business cards in case you misplaced the first one and want to talk to me when you heal. The doctor informed me you'll get better after six to eight weeks."

Lamar flushed the toilet. Afterward he came out the bathroom and sat on the chair next to Zenobia's bed.

"What's that pig's name? Never mind, I see her business card right here. I didn't want her to see me, that's why I took so long in the bathroom."

Tears fell down Zenobia's face.

"Whatever, you should leave with her and I should give in and call her because I'm tired of being tired."

Lamar put the card in his gray sweatpants pocket and sat on the chair.

"I'm sorry, I won't hit you again."

"That's what you told me when you broke my nose, so I don't want to be with you anymore. I'm going to ask Apollo Kidd to whoop your ass because you're weak, like your waves on your head."

Zenobia stared as she threw the pillow at him. Lamar blocked the pillow. He got down on one knee and poured his heart out.

"Okay, now you sound stupid about me getting my ass whooped. Listen, I'm so sorry. I didn't mean it. Please forgive me again, just one more time."

Zenobia's tears fell.

"Stop cryin' 'n hear me out. I … I don't know how to express my love, 'cause no one ever taught me how to love."

Zenobia started rocking her body.

"Oh my god it hurts when I talk. First, you must love yourself, then it would be easier to love me or anyone else."

Lamar stood up and rubbed his head.

"I used to watch my father abuse my mother when I was a little boy."

Zenobia signaled for Lamar to come closer to her.

"Sit on the bed with me. You need to end the cycle immediately because domestic violence is not love, and I can't take any more of your abuse."

Lamar shed a tear and got back down on one knee.

"Okay, I'll stop hittin' you then. Will you marry me 'n be my wife? I want you to be my wife. I want to have a kid with you … I can only afford one more since I already have six by six different women."

Zenobia thought, *I already know about his children he doesn't take care of. I hope he gets a job because unemployment doesn't last forever.*

Still, she forgave him because she believed the baby would brighten their relationship. Although her mind growled *NO*, she decided to follow her heart.

"Yes, I'll be your wife, but please don't ever hit me again. If you put your hands on me again, I'll kill you. I mean it."

Lamar stood up.

"Thank you."

When they went home it felt like the first day they met at the park. Lamar started treating her like his queen again. Zenobia wanted to tell Jada about the engagement, but she had moved the day after Zenobia went to the hospital because she didn't want to witness another domestic violence case. That night Zenobia and Lamar took a shower together. Lamar was serious about a new child.

"Don't forget, only one baby. After that I want you to get your tubes tied or take birth control pills."

It took six tries before Zenobia got pregnant. She was so stressed about trusting Lamar and that's why it took so long for her eggs to ovulate. She thought she was fertile, but unfortunately, nervousness played a huge factor. Zenobia kept second guessing herself. All sorts of negative thoughts filled her mind. Eventually, she became optimistic again and believed having a baby would change him and make their relationship better.

During the first month of pregnancy, Zenobia was excited. Finally, she would have someone she could call her own. The thought of being a mother made her smile every day. She felt she was in a pleasant place at that point of her life, and finally about to live the life she truly deserved. Maybe she was too happy for Lamar because he became extremely aggressive, insecure, and jealous. The saying is true: "Good things don't last forever." Because, as usual, they went right back to arguing and fighting again.

One morning Lamar pushed Zenobia onto the stairs. She fell on the steps and he raised his foot to kick her in the stomach. Zenobia covered her belly with both hands.

"Lamar, stop! You're hurting me!"

His insecurities caused him to get mad about a stranger talking to her at the mall the day before when they were out shopping for maternity and baby clothes. Zenobia was so excited about the pregnancy that she started preparing early.

"Lamar, the baby! Please don't hurt our baby! You promised me. Boy, if you cause me to have a miscarriage, I will slaughter you. I put that on everything I love!"

Amazingly, he tilted his head as he pinched his chin twice. Instead of kicking Zenobia, he helped her up and walked her to the bedroom.

Throughout her pregnancy, Zenobia prayed. Some months later, she was blessed with a healthy baby girl. Her newborn weighed eight pounds and five ounces. Zenobia named her Ty-Janae.

Once she had given birth, Lamar ranted.

"Get yo' tubes tied ASAP because I don't want any mo' kids."

"No, I'll just take the birth control pills instead, just in case you decide to change your mind."

The day Ty-Janae came home from the hospital, Zenobia decided to call Mary and asked her to come see her granddaughter.

I hope she's not mad at me for taking so long to check up on her.

(Phone rings)

"Hello, how are you Mom?"

"Use your inside voice, Pudge, I'm on the phone with your sister. I'm good Zee, nice to hear your voice. How are you?"

"I been going through a lot because I chose to be stubborn versus listening to you. Well, I have a baby and I named her Ty-Janae. I want you to meet her."

"Congratulations, I'm so happy for you! I'll be there in about an hour."

(Doorbell rings)

"Who is it? Stop covering the peephole."

"It's me."

"Hello, I know, I just had to make sure. Stop acting like a stranger and come inside."

"Wow let me take my shoes off because I don't want to get your shiny cherry red hardwood floor dirty."

"Cut it out, Mom, I know how to sweep and mop. I take my shoes off because of the germs. I don't want the nasty bacteria from outside to spread in the house."

"Okay, I understand. So, where's my grandbaby?"

Zenobia pointed.

"She's over there in the crib sleep. Her lazy father in the room sleep, too."

Marry noticed Zenobia's ring and instantly got upset. She switched seats to sit next to Zenobia.

"Nice ring, but why wasn't I invited to the ceremony?"

"Mom, we got married at City Hall, and I wasn't comfortable introducing either one of you."

Mary held Zenobia's hands.

"Did he make you do this? Is he manipulative? Is he controlling? Does he call you names? Does he put his hands on you? I know how jealous, insecure, and immature some men are."

"Mom, can we please change the subject? Honest, I don't want to talk about my husband because he may wake up soon."

Mary knew something was wrong. She noticed the way her daughter was holding back and being stubborn as always.

"I can respect that. Don't forget you still have a room for rent at my house whenever you want to get away from that boy of yours because he's not a man since I didn't meet him yet."

"Huh, for rent?"

"Just kidding, you have a room here for you and my first grand to share whenever you are ready. Zenobia, always remember, never put all your trust in a man. If you want anything done right, you must do it yourself because people are known for giving up and leaving you to struggle."

(Baby crying)

"Let me go spoil her precious behind."

Mary walked to Ty-Janae's crib and picked her up.

"Aww, I see you smelled grandma coming. Here I am, baby. How are you? Are you hungry? Welcome to this world full of crazy people. I'm your grandma and I love you so much. You're brightening up my day already with your brown eyes and big cheeks."

Ty-Janae went for Mary's breast.

"Zee, I see you breastfeed because she thinks I have milk in my breast."

Zenobia took Ty-Janae from Mary and smiled.

"Yes, doing my best to keep her healthy. Let me feed my greedy baby girl."

Mary kissed Ty-Janae before she gave her to Zenobia.

"I'm about to leave since your husband may wake up."

"Okay, Mother, his name is Lamar. I guess you'll meet him next time. Oh, tell my siblings I miss them. Wait, I love them, too. I'll visit soon."

"Okay, but you should visit Shante ASAP because she's been depressed. Rose is always busy with her best friend next door. Pudge is finally eighteen, so he thinks he's grown. I think he watch porn or something on YouTube. He better not get any hot ass girl pregnant. Hopefully Ty-Janae can bring happiness to our family and help us grow stronger together. I better see you and my precious baby before she turns five."

"Mom, you stay with jokes. I'll check up on Shante. Lock the bottom lock and thanks for visiting. Get home safely, and I love y'all."

Zenobia went through postpartum depression, feeling unhappy and having mood swings. It took her almost one year to visit her family. When Ty-Janae was eight months old, Zenobia decided she wanted her to have a sister or brother to play with. She never told Lamar about her decision. Instead she lied to him and pretended she was taking birth control pills. He noticed she was getting fat, but she blamed it on the side effects of those pills.

One day Zenobia finally had the courage to visit Mary's house so her siblings could finally see their niece.

(Phone rings)

Who's calling me from this number? They better leave a message because I hate people playing on my phone. Good, they left a message. Now let me see who just called.

(Voicemail)

Hi mom, it's me. Call me back this my new number.

My daughter finally reached out to me so let me call her back.

"Hello, how are you Mom?"

"I'm okay, Zee, how are you? I was worried about you since the day I left your house almost a year ago. I been calling and leaving voicemails. One day I called, and it said you had a new number. I was wondering when you were going to give me your new number."

"I'm doing my best to maintain. It's not easy basically raising a child on my own because Lamar is barely here. Then when he's here he wants to sleep or argue. I leave the house with Ty-Janae every chance I get."

"Hold on, let me put my wig on real quick."

"Mom, you are too young for wigs. You have hair, so you don't need a wig."

"Stop laughing, I put a wig on when I don't feel like doing my hair. If anyone is too young it's your generation because they wear more wigs than me, so hold on."

"All right."

"Okay I'm back. I tried to check on you by coming to your house, but your car wasn't there so I went on about my business and waited to hear from you. I'm happy you're alive because I have a bad feeling about Lamar, especially since I didn't meet him yet."

"Mom, let me put you on speaker phone so I could change Ty-Janae's pamper."

"Okay."

"Honest, I'm tired of him. Mom, I don't see us making it together much longer. Ty-Janae needs a sibling to play with, so I'll have one more child with him, then I'm done with this marriage."

"Zee, why have another child with him when he don't do his part with Ty-Janae? Listen, life is choices. You must make the best of you and my grandbaby life no matter who's there or not."

"I want my children to have the same father. I'm afraid to meet another man like Lamar, so I'd rather deal with him versus two of him. Can I come visit? I need to get me and my baby out this house before Lamar gets back."

"Come now because I'm going to the dentist in twenty minutes. Shante would be home alone and could use some company since she doesn't like people staring at her in the wheelchair."

"I'll head over there in about thirty-five minutes. Not sure if I'll be there when you get back from the dentist though because it's sad how they give everyone the same appointment time."

"You're right, they stay doing that then wonder why people

complain and have an attitude with them. Let me go because I'm not rescheduling."

"Okay, I love you and stay safe. I'm about to call Shante."

"Hello, how are you sis? Mommy told me you're about to call from your new number. Is my niece one now?"

"Hello, she's eight months. Tay don't fall asleep because I'm on my way. Stay close by the door."

"Cool! See you soon."

Once Zenobia got to the house she knocked on the door because the doorbell didn't work. When Shante opened the door, Zenobia placed Ty-Janae on Shante's lap and gave her a hug.

"What's going on? Nice seeing you Tay. Let's go inside so you can enjoy your niece."

Shante was all smiles.

"Hi, I'm aunt Tay-Tay. You are gorgeous."

Shante kissed Ty-Janae on both cheeks.

"Sis, lock the bottom lock and push me by the rocking chair."

Zenobia did as told then put the baby bag on the living room table and sat in the rocking chair.

Shante locked her wheels and glanced at Zenobia.

"Damn, I miss you and I see yo' booty pokin' out."

Zenobia snickered.

"I miss you more. Stop with that Gay junk and focus on my daughter before you drop her. She'll be one in two months and I'm thinking about throwing her a party here in the backyard. She's almost walking, too."

Before Shante could respond, Zenobia threw up for the second time in less than an hour. Also, she had vomited before she got there.

"Sis, are you okay?"

Zenobia ran to the bathroom and slammed the door. After she took care of her business she headed back to the living room.

"Are you okay?"

Zenobia bent over and held her stomach.

"Tay, I'm good. That darn fast food messed my stomach up."

Shante stared with that 'get the hell out of here who do you think you're fooling' face. She twisted her lips to the side.

"Girl, bye! Yo' ass knocked up again."

Quickly, Zenobia got defensive.

"Shante don't play with me. For one, stop cursing in front of my baby. For two, you know darn well I don't play all of them baby games. Mommy put up a fight raising us, so no thank you. Who in this day and era has time or money for more than one child? I'm struggling taking care of Ty-Janae because her father is useless."

"Damn, you all extra and shit, oops, I meant stuff … Oh, now you calling me Shante? What happened to Tay or Sis? Don't get no damn attitude wit' me! Hell, I would hope you not that dumb to have another baby by that sorry ass niggah. We weren't even invited to the wedding. I never want to meet him either. I don't have any respect for that clown."

"My fault, I was wrong for not having any of you there. I let him talk me into going to City Hall. He claimed he didn't want to wait another day to get married."

Ty-Janae had fallen asleep, so Shante passed her to Zenobia.

"Feed my niece before she wakes up crying."

"Give me my baby and finish speaking your mind because I see you have a lot more to say."

Shante unlocked her wheelchair and went to the kitchen to warm her shrimp and broccoli in the microwave. When she finished, she went back in the living room.

"I heard about Lamar, and um, I know he didn't change. I know you are the oldest, but I know marriage, or a baby won't change a *boy*. Clearly he's not a man."

Ty-Janae started moving her head, so Zenobia started rocking her in the rocking chair.

"What did you hear about him and what do you mean by he didn't change?"

Shante ate a shrimp and some broccoli.

"You better let da homies whoop on his ass like he whips on yours."

Zenobia started rocking a little faster in the rocking chair.

"No, didn't you leave that gang life behind you?"

Shante ate another shrimp and more broccoli.

"Yes, I put my flag down and don't gang bang anymore, but I still know some of the shooters who stay ready for war. Lamar hits you, right? Don't lie to me either, because he's known for hitting women. I bet he started abusing you when you tried to get him to meet us."

"Actually, I beat him up now. I had boxing lessons a few months ago from Apollo Kidd. Lamar tries to calm me down because he knows I won't tolerate that BS from him anymore."

"That's what all battered women say. Wait, let me guess, he's not going to hit you again and he loves you ... Right?"

Zenobia almost threw up again. She didn't want to talk about Lamar any longer.

"Here, hold your niece."

Shante ate the last bit of her food, put the empty platter on the chair, and reached her arms out.

"Give her to me before you throw up on her."

Zenobia threw Shante's empty platter in the kitchen garbage then went to the bathroom.

"Zee, hurry and clean the lies out your mouth so you can come back in here and tell me the truth. When the last time Lamar hit you? Did you tell Mommy? If not, I'm telling when she gets back from the dentist. Oh, and I'm telling her you're pregnant."

As Zenobia gargled and rinsed the funny taste out her mouth, she thought, *Typical Shante, always ready for drama. She didn't even think to let me get myself together before she started running her mouth. Well, I must admit she is speaking facts. Yes, the saying is true: the truth hurts.*

On her way back to the living room, Zenobia decided to go home because she needed rest. The unborn baby was draining her. She was six weeks pregnant. Zenobia told Shante everything before she left.

Morning sickness was no joke. Zenobia couldn't keep anything down. Dealing with her husband didn't make it any better. She preferred sleeping than arguing with Lamar.

Zenobia woke up after her nap and heard Lamar playing a video game. He was so loud talking to the television that she thought he had company. She peeked in the living room and noticed he was drinking Coors Light beer plus some type of dark liquor. She headed back in her room to write in her diary.

Dear Diary,

Lamar and Coors Light beer don't mix well at all. The last time he drank two of them beers he broke my jaw. Now he's drinking it with liquor. Please pray for me. Pray that this night will be an okay night because I can't deal with another dispute. I'm starting to think I was safer and happier in the street. Sadly, when Shante got stabbed, I was thinking about retaliation when I should have called the cops. When she got paralyzed, I considered a bigger plot. I still hear the gun sound from when I got shot. I had the streets hot. It caught up to me and I was forced to stop.

POEM

Painful

I miss when he used to hold me yes, caress
I hate when he hit me and cause me stress
He was my favorite
Number one hero
Now I'm full of regrets
He's just a nightmare pure evil

CHAPTER ELEVEN

Final Strike

As Zenobia headed to the kitchen, Lamar barked.

"Damn, you finally got yo' lazy ass up. Shit, it's damn near 7 PM and I don't smell shit cookin'."

That man's whole life consisted of cursing. Zenobia rolled her eyes and put the turkey wings in the oven that she had marinated the night before. She sat at the table and chopped up some cheese for the macaroni. Her phone went off. She knew it was Mary by the ring tone she had set for her.

"It's your mother calling you."

Zenobia always laughed when she heard that. Unfortunately, she couldn't smile … She let the phone ring because she knew Shante ran her mouth, and the last thing she needed to hear was Mary's tough love. Mary's call went to voicemail, and of course she left a message. Zenobia just wasn't in a rush to check it. She decided to turn the television on to the gospel channel instead. She never attended church, so gospel music was her stress reliever.

"This is for that little child with no father …" Her song came right on time, so she started singing with the music. Zenobia loved "Lean on Me" by Kirk Franklin. She swore some songs were written specifically for her. As she was in her spiritual zone, cooking and playing music, there came Lucifer AKA Lamar.

"Damn, you in here worshippin' and shit. Bitch, I'm starvin' and it don't take 'dat fucking long to bake no turkey wings and macaroni."

"Bae, I'm sorry. Five more minutes, I promise."

When he left the kitchen, she hurried and finished cooking. She made his plate and Ty-Janae's, too. She couldn't eat because the baby was craving tuna fish with cheese, so she made it and sat in the kitchen and ate alone.

As soon as she thought the night was going to end well, Lamar came in the kitchen with his ignorance.

"Bitch, since when you fuckin' pregnant?"

Lamar held her phone in his hand.

"You told me 'dem pills have you feeling nauseous and gainin' weight and shit. I told yo' dumb ass how many children to have. You may think I'm stupid, but I know yo' triflin' ass would be like 'da rest of 'dem stupid bitches and run to child support on me."

Zenobia forgot to check Mary's message, but nosy behind Lamar had no problem checking it for her. If she would have told him 'don't touch my phone,' he would have assumed she was cheating on him. Lamar continued to go off and call her all sorts of disrespectful, degrading names. He was on his way to the living room, but he came back in the kitchen.

"You really tryna' play wit' me, right?"

Before she could deny it, he punched her in the mouth. Zenobia tasted the blood instantly. She reacted with a jab and uppercut.

Lamar was so mad her punches connected.

"Oh bitch, you still want to fight back. I think I have to remind you of last time, but this time ya' gettin' a double dose. I'm gonna whoop you and 'dat baby's ass. Bitch, I'm gonna beat 'dat baby out of yo' ass."

As he went to swing again, Zenobia took the lamp and swung it with all her might and cracked him in his head with it. When she tried to sprint away, he pulled her by the ankles. She fell hard. He kicked her in the stomach. Zenobia cried out. She was weak and in so much discomfort, she couldn't guard herself. Kick after kick after kick, she just laid on the floor and cried. She couldn't fight back anymore. She had no energy or tears left. Lamar stopped kicking Zenobia when he caught eye contact with Ty-Janae.

Ty-Janae screamed, and Zenobia crawled over to her and hugged her. She wanted to take that terrified look off her daughter's face.

"It's okay. Let's get ready for bed."

Zenobia's abdominal pain felt like she was in labor. The cramps felt like flashes of lightning had struck her stomach. Once she managed to get up and put Ty-Janae to bed, Zenobia went to the bathroom and released a bloody stool. *Oh my God!* She called the ambulance and went to the emergency room because she was afraid. She wanted to make sure her baby was okay, but she was in too much misery to drive. To her knowledge, she believed the baby was moving and kicking as normal. Unfortunately, the doctor confirmed that she had a miscarriage instead.

Devastated by the doctor's news, she thought of committing suicide. Then she thought, *Before I kill myself, I'm going to assassinate Lamar.* Not only was she physically in pain, her mental was taking a hard beating as well. Never in her life had she felt so much pain. Zenobia was fed up. The senseless loss of a child was worse than anything; but she wanted another child. Having another baby father was not an option either. She never held any hatred in her heart until Lamar mentally, emotionally, verbally, and physically abused her. Angrier than she had ever been, rage filled her heart and revenge took over her mind. Zenobia's only thought was murdering Lamar. She was seconds away from putting a price on his head. She had shooters that would have done the dirty work for free. She didn't start his life, however, she wanted to put an end to it. She wanted his sorry behind dead that night.

Mary spoke in her head, interrupting the murderous thoughts. *Zenobia, always remember ... never put all your trust in a man. If you want anything done right, you must do it yourself because people are known for giving up and leaving you to struggle.*

Zenobia knew how the streets talked, so she didn't want any witnesses involved. People claim they can keep a secret and won't snitch. It's a different situation when federal agents arrest them for homicide. Once a prison sentence of thirty years to life for first degree murder is imposed, the average person would tell. Therefore, Zenobia decided to take matters into her own hands. Zenobia planned her alibi and thought of a possible story to tell just in case she got caught. Embarrassingly, everyone knew how Lamar beat her, so she figured self-defense was the perfect explanation, and if that didn't work, she would ask for a plea bargain. What that punk put her through during the two years they lived together was well worth serving life without the possibility of parole.

Zenobia realized the saying was true: "you never know a person until you move in together." She believed karma was real and what goes around comes around. She wanted revenge quick, fast, and in a hurry. She got on her cellular phone and started doing her homework on the best ways to murder someone without getting caught. She accumulated a lot of information from the Internet, such as how to make it look like a suicide and destroy the evidence; slip drugs into his beverage or food to make it look like an overdose; kill him on a cruise ship and dump his body overboard; wear gloves and shoes that are too big, then make it look like a robbery. The possibilities were endless and the fact that Lamar robbed her baby of his or her life made her more than willing to go to jail for taking his life. Zenobia was on a serious mission.

When she went back home, Lamar was at the kitchen table with an ice pack on his head. Zenobia didn't feel sorry for him. She stood over him and whispered, "You one-minute little-penis jerk. You caused me to have a miscarriage."

She spoke softly because she didn't want to wake Ty-Janae up. It was payback time. Before he could say a word, she punched him in his eye, then kicked him in his testicles. He yelped like a howling dog. Lamar dropped the ice pack, fell to the black and white tile floor, and held one hand over his eye and the other on his balls.

Zenobia was filled with so much anger that she hit Lamar continuously until his face was bloody.

"Now it's your turn to have a broken nose and jaw."

Lamar was hurting so bad that he couldn't fight back. Zenobia was trying to kill him, but then she suddenly stopped to let him talk.

"I—"

Lamar was trying to say something. She wasn't sure if he wanted to say, "I'm sorry," "I love you," or "I'm dying." He had gone too far. Zenobia wouldn't let anything change her decision to leave him there to suffer. She spat in his face. She didn't bother to call the ambulance. It felt so good for her to finally have him in a painful predicament. Once she got tired of looking at him, she woke her daughter up and they left the house. It was very important that Ty-Janae have her father in her life, but Zenobia refused to continue being a fool and stay in an abusive relationship. As she drove off to a new beginning, a few thoughts came to her. *We live in a dog eat dog world. Life is like a game of chess—plan your next move. That was the final strike!*

Before Zenobia woke Ty-Janae up to go to Mary's house she decided to sit at the kitchen table and wrote a poem.

Dear Diary,

I wish I had the courage to say this to Lamar.

POEM

Fed Up

I'm so lost I don't know where this is going

This must stop because our relationship isn't growing

I'm losing my sight and I can't see what's ahead

If I stay I'll end up dead

You claim you love me, it doesn't show

I wish this pain would go I'm not a smut, jump off, or whore

I'm fed up with you beating and throwing me on the floor

Your time is up. You must go.

You're not worth my tears and the one who is won't make me cry

I'm hurt, but through it all I'm still going to hold my head up high

I hope you learn your lesson from this, or you'll end up with a domestic violence charge

Love don't live here anymore, you're about to starve

CHAPTER TWELVE

Trust Issues

Zenobia was losing every piece of trust in men, so she decided to seek out a female psychiatrist. She made it her business to speak to a woman and not a man. Zenobia's eyebrows started to sweat as she signed in for her first therapy session.

"Hello, have a seat Zenobia Jordan, and you'll be seen shortly."

Zenobia wiped her eyebrows.

"Hi, how did you know my name?"

"Well, I read the sign-in sheet because that's what I'm paid to do. By the way, nice leopard blouse."

"Thank you, and you're right. Please forgive me because I've never been here before."

"I know. It's okay, you'll feel better once you talk to Dr. Bryant."

"Uhh … may I have some water?"

"Sure, then have a seat until you're called."

"Thank you."

Zenobia proceeded to get a cup of water from the water dispenser. She sat down and drank her water as she faced the television in the waiting room. She wasn't paying attention to the images or voices on the screen because she had thoughts of rescheduling her appointment.

"Zenobia Jordan."

Zenobia stood up and threw her cup in the garbage. She noticed the patch of gray in the doctor's curls. Also, her beautiful diamond ring.

"Coming."

"How are you? I'm Dr. Bryant and before you ask, no, I'm not married to Kobe Bryant. But I love watching him play. Follow me to my office."

As she walked behind Dr. Bryant, Zenobia looked in each room.

"That's amazing because the Lakers are my favorite team."

Dr. Bryant walked in her office then sat in the chair behind her desk.

"Nice to know you're a basketball fan."

Zenobia examined Dr. Bryant's office. She was impressed with the big plaques on the wall. Most impressive were the two different bachelor's degrees.

"Yes, I love sports. I'm a Lakers, New Jersey Devils, New York Mets, and New York Giants fan. Sadly, my life's been so complicated that I don't have time to do anything I love."

Dr. Bryant smiled at Kobe Bryant's rookie card on her desk.

"Have a seat, Zenobia, and let's get to business."

Zenobia sat on the brown sofa.

"Loosen up and relax. We'll be here for about an hour."

A teardrop fell.

"Are you okay? We don't have to stay the full hour if you're not comfortable."

Zenobia wiped the side of her face as more tears started to fall.

"I'm okay."

"I'm not here to judge, so you need to be open with me and let the stress out."

"This couch reminds me of the one I had when I used to live with Lamar, but it was black. He used to hit me every chance he got."

Dr. Bryant leaned forward and put her elbows on the desk.

"Who is Lamar?"

"Lamar is my daughter's father."

"Sorry to hear that. Are you still in a relationship with him?"

"No, I hate him, and I don't want another man because between him and my father, I'm not sure what men are good for … that's why I have trust issues."

Dr. Bryant sat back in her chair.

"Oh no. Can you tell me a little bit more about your dad?"

Zenobia took a deep breath and decided to vent some more.

"Can I take my shoes off?"

Dr. Bryant nodded.

"Yes, as long as they don't stink."

Zenobia forced a smile.

"Good one."

She took her shoes off and made herself comfortable.

"Well, my life experiences caused me to keep my guard up since I never knew what anyone was capable of. Every time I decided to trust someone, I got hurt. People may never fully understand why or how I developed trust issues. It started when I was a young girl who kept waiting for my father to be a willing participant in my life. The lies and broken promises ended my desire to trust anyone. I figured if I couldn't trust him, then how could I trust anyone else, especially a stranger? At the end of the day, people lie, numbers don't."

Dr. Bryant reached for her pen to take notes.

"You're doing good, continue to express your feelings."

Zenobia crossed her legs.

"So much has happened that left me skeptical about people. Real talk, I've been through so much in my life that no one could walk one step in my shoes. I never understood anyone who makes a promise and doesn't keep it. All I ever wanted was for a person to say what they mean and mean what they say. Like my mother always says, 'Keep it one hundred.' That phrase was so true. All anyone has at the end of the day is their word. It's simple: say yes or no, and if you're not sure, then say so."

"I hear you, but what if saying yes or no isn't simple for others? What if they were only taught to say what would appease another person for their own benefit, or to prevent the other person from being hurt by the truth? I'm curious, what are your thoughts on that?"

Zenobia uncrossed her legs.

"Individuals are human and not perfect, therefore, they're liable to be deceitful and untrustworthy. No matter what I still prefer the truth even if it hurts."

"That's a great point, Zenobia. Meanwhile, in life we can't be afraid to trust anyone. However, we must be careful whom we trust. Through actions, a person reveals if he or she deserves trust."

"Well, there you have it. Growing up without my father active in my life caused a lot of hurt and pain, and Lamar's abusive ways added to it, Doc'. Honest, it's not easy to get over."

Dr. Bryant took more notes.

"Wow, that's a lot to soak in. Exactly how do you feel about your father?"

Zenobia shrugged her shoulders.

"I don't have any feelings about him. Sometimes I wish he was dead or in jail because I understand the logic behind a parent not being active in their child's life because of those reasons."

Dr. Bryant held the ink pen to her chin.

"Are you sure?"

Zenobia put her head down while she twirled her dreadlocks around her finger.

"Yes, that's the only way I would understand why he's not part of my life."

"Your tears show a lot more than you're telling me."

Zenobia grabbed some tissue from the arm of the sofa. After that she started putting her shoes on.

"I don't feel like talking anymore. Can I leave?"

Dr. Bryant stood up and walked over to Zenobia.

"Sure, just settle your payment first."

Zenobia handed Dr. Bryant a one-hundred-dollar bill.

"Should I give this to you or the receptionist?"

Dr. Bryant reached in her pocket and handed Zenobia a fifty-dollar bill.

"I'll take care of it because my next client is not arriving until about two hours. Here, since you didn't stay the full hour. Let me get you a receipt."

"Thank you."

Dr. Bryant went to her desk and filled out a receipt, then gave it to Zenobia.

"Okay, now you're good. I'll see you next week for your second session, just call me or my secretary tomorrow so we can set a date and time since you have a lot on your mind now. Also, I'm going to evaluate you. The evaluation is going to help me provide you with great services."

"Thank you, and how do I get out again?"

Dr. Bryant walked Zenobia to the doorway and pointed toward the left.

"Go this way and you see that second door? Turn right and the elevators are on the opposite side across the hall."

Zenobia rushed out the elevator and power walked to her car. Although she knew it was best to see Dr. Bryant again, Zenobia didn't know if she would go back. She didn't think she could handle Dr. Bryant seeing her cry again. Zenobia had six days to think about it. She had a lot on her mind so before she left the parking lot, she grabbed her notebook from the glove compartment.

Dear Diary,

Give me the courage to vent to that shrink next week because I feel like an emotional rollercoaster. Also, help me so I'm brave enough to turn my journal entries into a book one day. I'm willing to relive the pain once more to better someone else's life. I'm on a mission to prevent the youth from making the same mistakes I made. I'm determined to impact lives, and I will make a difference for the better.

POEM

Traumatized

It's no secret stop the fuss

No, I don't trust

Before you judge me listen up matter of fact hush

I must be comfortable and happy all the time that's a must

Everyone I tried to trust did me wrong

They either lied to me or stole from me so I don't trust one soul

Time supposed to heal all wounds, so I've been told

If I could do it all over again I wouldn't have Lamar as a boyfriend all he ever did was lie to me and abuse me

Eventually he would have killed me

I would never be able to trust again

CHAPTER THIRTEEN

Moment of Hope

Zenobia dropped to her knees because she was upset about the test results from her evaluation. *Ahhh! I can't take it. I'm trying to live right, but it's always something. What is going on with me? Am I getting punished for my past? Is this Karma? I need to spend more time with my mother and siblings before I lose my min*d.

Lord please, I don't know the correct way to pray, and I never asked you for much of anything. I'm finally down on both knees begging you for help. I want to repent. Will you forgive me for my sins? Can you help me? I need help, and I want help. They say the first sign is admitting ... This is my moment of hope, so don't let me down. I can't keep going through life not trusting people. I'm one hundred percent sure it's not going to be an easy journey. Honestly, I'm truly willing to try it before I die. It may help control my impulsive type ADHD. I may never mention it to anyone, but that shrink diagnosed me with ADHD. She even prescribed me Ritalin, but I never filled my prescription since I believe in natural cures. I'm hyper and I know by keeping busy I'll maintain without medicine because the side effects are ridiculous. I want to know how it feels to trust a person whole heartedly because I've never experienced it before. I made a mistake trying to trust Lamar when I didn't trust myself.

Zenobia had serious trust issues to the point she counted her money when it came out the ATM. Throughout her journey she had met a few good people in her life. For example, during elementary school she met a wonderful community woman and anger management mentor by the name of Skillz. She taught Zenobia a lot about the real world, especially how tough black women have it. It was nice having someone like her in her life. She wished their friendship would have lasted longer. It was Zenobia's fault though. She wanted to build a relationship like that with her father instead of a stranger. At the time she didn't understand strangers can love you more than your family. Well, that part of her life was finally behind her. Now, she finally accepted the things she couldn't change. Her glimpse into the mirror helped her understand that she was ready to change for the better. Zenobia understood the timing was wrong, and it was meant for her to go through life lessons on her own. She decided to create a Facebook account and find Skillz. Zenobia believed they would reunite again and stay in contact forever.

POEM

Strength

Asking for help is a sign of strength

I'm weak and crying out

I cried more than I laughed yes, I'm sad

I'm barely standing on my own two feet

I lost my appetite I don't remember my last bite

All I do is get upset and want to argue and fight

I know that's not right

Hello strength are you there

I've been looking for you everywhere

Can you help me make that fear disappear

It constantly whoops my behind over and over again

I must put this to an end I'm determined to win

CHAPTER FOURTEEN

Quality Time

Zenobia realized she might never get to know her father, so she decided to cherish her mother and siblings. Sometimes Zenobia thought about how much of a woman her mother Mary really was. Her mother wasn't a smoker, she drank socially, and had never been behind bars. Mary taught Zenobia that life was all about choices, and it's up to each person to make the best out of life, no matter who's there.

People usually said, "A woman can't play both parental roles." Zenobia used to beg to differ since her mother didn't do such a bad job with her without James' help. Although Mary showed Zenobia tough love, she always had clothes, food, and a roof over her head. After analyzing her life, Zenobia agreed it took two to create her, therefore, it should have been two raising her. No matter how much her mother loved her, she always wanted to build a relationship with her dad. Additionally, no matter how much she claimed she wish James was dead or in jail, deep down she was crying out for attention to build a relationship with him. Sure, Mary was the only parent she knew, and Mary attempted to be both parents wrapped up in one. Unfortunately, she couldn't give Zenobia the love and attention she wanted from James. With that fact, she lived life as a fatherless child.

One day Zenobia left Dr. Bryant's office feeling like a new

woman. She called Mary with a big smile.

"Mom, how are you?"

"Hello, I'm good."

Zenobia put her seatbelt on.

"I'm on my way to take you all to my favorite food spot. It's important that we spend quality time with each other."

Mary rubbed her stomach.

"You're right, it's important for our family. How are we going to fit with Ty-Janae's car seat in the car?"

"I took it out because she's with the babysitter."

Mary removed her hand from her belly and placed it on her waist.

"Huh? Babysitter?"

"I wasn't hiding my personal problems from you, but I've been seeing a psychiatrist for a month. I'll talk to you about it another day."

"Okay, come pick us up. See you soon."

The phone call ended then Zenobia drove to pick her family up.

"Mom, do you remember why Amari's Diner is my favorite?" Zenobia asked as the entire family sat enjoying a meal.

"The breakfast, right? Wait, the sports theme, too?"

Zenobia showed all her teeth.

"Yes, especially because they serve breakfast twenty-four seven here."

The nourishment was delicious. Zenobia loved to customize her pancakes with banana and blueberries. They were having a great time until she witnessed a group of teenagers throwing away food. She flashed back to the increasing homeless population in her city and immediately jumped out her chair and stormed over toward them.

"Why aren't you eating your food? It's a lot of bums outside who would love it!"

The individuals looked at each other to see who would respond first.

"Zee, get back over here and mind your business."

"Mom, someone needs to knock some sense in these ungrateful youngsters today."

All the customers stared at Zenobia and the teenagers by the garbage can.

Zenobia glanced at Mary then back at the young people.

"Mom, it takes a village."

Mary glanced at her children. Rose was busy on Facebook. Pudge was fixated on a YouTube video. Shante was enjoying the show Zenobia was putting on.

"Zee, your siblings are watching you."

Zenobia ignored her and focused on speaking her mind without fighting and going to jail for hitting a minor. She stood in front of the door to get a message out before it was too late.

"Maybe y'all don't realize this, so allow me to spit some knowledge before y'all leave this joint. Pay attention and school others every chance you get. It's homeless people out there who wish they could have the food that was thrown in the garbage. Y'all inconsiderate, selfish, ungrateful, unappreciative behinds won't understand until you're outside hungry and thirsty."

One of the children pointed.

"Go in da' garbage and get da' food then, captain-save-a-meal."

Zenobia swallowed her spit.

Of course, it's always a difficult person in the group.

Mary stood up.

"Zee, for the last time, get back over here before we get kicked out."

It took everything in her to keep her composure, then she just walked away. As Zenobia and Mary sat down, Shante snickered.

Zenobia folded her arms on the table and stared at Shante.

"Are you okay? I don't find anything funny about throwing food in the garbage."

Shante giggled harder.

"True, but the captain-save-a-meal part was funny."

Zenobia looked at Rose and Pudge to see if they were laughing, too. Then her attention went back at Shante.

"You're still laughing. Well, you hurt my feelings. You're entertaining them disrespectful teenagers, which is making me extremely embarrassed. Mommy thought about aborting me, but she should have swallowed that nut or had an abortion instead of having you."

"What did you say?"

"I said …"

Mary interrupted.

"Zee, you better apologize and watch your damn mouth."

"I don't appreciate you laughing at me in front of strangers, payback is coming, Shante. Believe that."

Zenobia was a tit for tat woman. She knew two wrongs didn't make a right—well, in her eyes two wrongs made an even. Before Zenobia thought about a way to humiliate Shante, she reminded her about their life growing up.

"Did you forget about those nights I tried to throw pig feet, pork chops, and other food in the garbage because it was disgusting to me?"

Shante wanted to laugh.

"No."

"Well, do you remember how much you hated eating liver and salad? In case you forgot, Mommy was so mad she took us outside and made us watch homeless people dig in the garbage for something to eat. Since I'm the oldest, I remember."

"Yeah, I…"

Mary interfered.

"Cut it out right now because we're making a big scene. We

can talk about this somewhere else. I'm shocked you still remember that anyway. Believe it or not, I didn't think you cared, Zee."

"Mom, I felt bad for homeless people ever since that day. I'll always care. I won't ever forget. At that moment I realized I'd do whatever it took so we'd never be in that situation. Also, I miss balling so I'm thinking about joining a team overseas and hopefully become a successful WNBA player one day. When the time comes, I'll make it my business to feed the homeless. Thank you for bringing that to my attention at a young age because it helped me to be grateful and appreciative in life."

Mary took a huge gulp of her orange juice.

"You're welcome, and I see you're passionate about it, but be careful when you approach people because everyone don't care and don't agree either. Let me pay and get us out of here safely before I catch a case. I'm tired of the extra eyes on us."

Zenobia pulled out some money.

"No, I'll pay."

Two weeks later, Zenobia treated Mary to the same restaurant because she needed bonding time for just the two of them.

"Mom, for too many years I held so much in, and I just want to vent and get some stuff off my chest. Thanks to my therapy sessions, expressing myself is easier."

Mary put her fork down and focused her attention on Zenobia.

"I'm all ears, so speak your mind."

Zenobia swallowed the pancake followed by two gulps of cranberry juice.

"Well, I started seeing a psychiatrist this year because I didn't want Ty-Janae to suffer from my childhood pain."

Mary reached for her drink and almost knocked the glass over.

"Don't tell me someone raped you!"

Zenobia poured more syrup on her pancakes.

"No, I was having suicidal thoughts and cried a lot. However, I must stay strong for my baby girl."

Mary spat her scrambled eggs and cheese out because she almost choked.

"Huh? You had what? How is it that you never told me?"

Zenobia drank some more cranberry juice, then exhaled.

"I was miserable and depressed, hoping, wishing, and praying to spend quality time with James. I used to feel like killing myself would take all my stress away."

Tears welled up. Mary folded her hands and looked into her daughter's eyes with intensity.

"Do you still feel like that?"

Zenobia smiled.

"Not at all, and that's why I'm speaking my truth. Dr. Bryant helped me understand a lot of adult pain comes from childhood hurt that was never healed."

"I can't believe you were going through so much because you pretended that everything was cool. I hope your siblings are not having suicidal thoughts."

"Mom, no disrespect, but why didn't you ever ask me how I felt about James not being in my life? I thought you didn't want to talk about it, so I kept my feelings hidden, which resulted in so much stress."

Mary's tears fell and went into her scrambled eggs and cheese.

"Believe it or not, I felt the same way, as if you didn't want to talk about it. I promise I did my best to play both parental roles. Thank you for being honest because it'll be easier for me to have this talk with your siblings."

Zenobia reached over the table and wiped Mary's tears.

"I understand, and I'm finally happy. I used to smile to keep from crying, and now I smile because I'm truly happy."

Mary dug in her handbag for some money.

"I'm happy to hear that. Let me pay since you paid last time."

Zenobia leaned back and put both hands above her head.

"Okay, are you taking your food to go?"

"Yes."

"I don't have much left. I'll just finish mine."

Mary put her food in a to-go container. Zenobia ate the last of her pancakes.

"Zee, are you okay? You look like you have more on your mind. Do you have anything else you want to talk about?"

Zenobia hesitated.

"Uh … Uh … Not really."

Mary put her container in the plastic bag.

"I'll take not really as a yes. You might as well go ahead, I'm listening. We'll sit here and talk until you're ready to go."

Zenobia drank the last of her cranberry juice.

"I can't believe I was in an abusive relationship. For some strange reason, I thought it was love."

Mary got up from her seat and sat next to Zenobia while placing one hand on Zenobia's lap.

"Zee don't beat yourself up about it. I'm happy you got out alive."

Zenobia placed her hand on her mother's and smiled.

"Thank you, Mom, for not judging me."

"No judgment, as long as you learned your lesson and don't let it happen again. Well, at least make sure you leave ASAP."

Zenobia's tears dropped.

"Yes, I learned my lesson, and I'll never settle again because love shouldn't hurt. I deserve someone who respects me and treats me like I mean the world to them. I'm going to take care of me and Ty-Janae and wait for my soulmate to find me. I am a beautiful queen."

Mary wiped Zenobia's tears.

"Good idea, but I hope Ty-Janae don't ask for a brother or sister soon."

Zenobia laughed.

"She better not. If she asks, I'll adopt a boy and name him Major, or a girl and name her Ja-Tya. Now let's go because we've been here too long."

Mary stood up with both arms out, then Zenobia rose to hug her mother.

"I love you so much, Zee."

"Mom, I love you more."

ACKNOWLEDGEMENTS

There is no "I" in "TEAM" and I'm blessed to have people in my life who pushed me to finish my book. Mommy (Rosemary Gibbs) I love you! You've always been everything to me, my confidante, friend, and number one fan; thank you. To my sisters Tyshimah and Octavia Gibbs, thank you for always having my back; I can honestly say that your first best friends are your siblings. I know without any doubts that I can depend on both of you. Most people don't understand the relationship I have with Erica, Malcolm, and Isaiah McNeil.

Although we don't have the same mother, I never felt like you loved me any less. Thank you for showing me compassion despite my relationship with our father.

To Haashim El-Amin and the entire IINNAC's Works family, thank you for believing in me and pushing me to another level of creativity. Zenobia, we been through a lot with our friendship, but we can count on each other and that says it all. A special thanks to My Tweety, words can't explain how much you mean to me well, I'll continue to do my best to show you because I love you so much.

Last but certainly not least, my guardian angels; my cousin Altriece and Grandma Mary Gibbs. It's not easy expressing the way I feel because I miss you both. I miss your voices, laughs, and I'm cherishing the many memories we shared. This book would not be possible without you, forever in my heart and always on my mind; may you both rest in peace.

ABOUT THE AUTHOR

Alethea Gibbs also known as Gibbs Truth was born on June 29, 1985 in Newark, NJ and raised in Irvington, NJ. Growing up without her biological father was tough for her, but it also forced her to become the woman she is today. In college she realized that creative writing was her outlet; it was the only thing that allowed her to feel completely free. Free from this world and the burdens she was dealing with. She graduated from New Jersey City University in 2009. Life didn't get easier after graduation; in fact, it became more of a challenge. She tried to find her career job, often felt constantly judged because of her lifestyle and she needed to escape reality. It was then that she was reminded of her passion for writing. I hope you enjoyed the reality and creativity that was put into her book. Please feel free to follow her on social media @GibbsTruth. She wants to build a relationship with her readers. Reach out via E-mail: GibbsTruth@hotmail.com
Website: www.gibbstruth.com

Gibbs Truth
PO Box 3624
Newark, NJ 07103

Made in the USA
Middletown, DE
14 April 2022

64236758R00086